YOURS SINCERELY

NOT A SELF HELP BOOK

SHEIKH MOHAMMAD AYAN HASAN

Dedicated to Mom and Dad.

<u>Special Thanks</u>-

Sheikh Mohammad Amaan Hasan

Adarsh Prakash

Shivang Pandey

Fayeq Qamar

Mohd Asif

and the folks at Notion Press.

Contents

Preface   *vii*

  1. Parents And Family   1

  2. Childhood And Teenage   12

  3. Relationship & Love   20

  4. Being A Muslim And Views On Religion   31

  5. News And Opinions   41

  6. Societal Rant   57

  7. Country: Expectations Vs Reality   78

  8. How To Pencil Out The Perfect Way For   103

    Existence?

  9. Life And The Issues Surrounding It   107

Finishing The Book   121

With Love   123

Preface

I wrote this book keeping in mind the nine things I wanted to talk about. I did not aim for it to be categorized as a self help book because it's not. Each chapter of this book deals with one particular aspect of life which I'm passionate about and want to write about. These chapters also reflect my views on the respective topics. Each chapter begins with a Bollywood movie dialogue which encapsulates the essence of the chapter. The tone of the chapters ranges from satire to serious. So, the reader's discretion is advised. I have tried my best to remain unbiased in my point of view. I don't mean to hurt anyone's sentiments. I have beeped out the swear words in case any minor is reading.

That's all,
Have a good read.

CHAPTER ONE

PARENTS AND FAMILY

"Aaj... aaj ek hasi aur baant lo, aaj ek dua aur maang lo, aaj ek ansoon aur pee lo, aaj ek zindagi aur jee lo, aaj ek sapna aur dekh lo. aaj ... kya pata, kal ho naa ho..."

My father's name is Sheikh Zafrul Hasan and my mom's name is Sheikh Shaheen Bano. They have been married for the past twenty-five years. My father used to be zari shop owner before he married my mother. When they got married, my mom thought of venturing into business. Being a highly educated and motivated woman, she thought of starting a school. My father agreed with her chain of thought. Back in the 1990s, education particularly in a densely populated Muslim dominated residential area was considered a dumb idea. Everyone used to learn some mechanical skill and earn their livelihood. Most of the people migrated to one of the Gulf nations for making money and other job prospects. The concept of educating oneself and getting a desk job or running a big business wasn't something that the samaaj accepted. My mother and father got a loan, sold some jewellery and established a school. The school was named S. B. MODERN EDUCATION CENTRE. The school started functioning in April of 1996. It's been more than twenty-five years and both my parents are still very much at it. Still motivated as ever and going one day at a time.

Going into some history now. My father belongs to a small rural village called Tickwamau. It lies around a hundred and twenty kilometres far from Lucknow. He was the eldest son in the family. Since my grandfather had a reputed job in the Indian Railways, he was usually posted in different cities until his retirement. Hence, my father spent much of his childhood and teenage years in my grandfather's absence. He came to Lucknow after completing his Under-Graduation and set up a small business here. On the other hand, my mother was born in Lucknow. She has been an urban dweller since birth unlike my father. She completed her college and got married to my father at the age of 21.

Patriarchy 101.

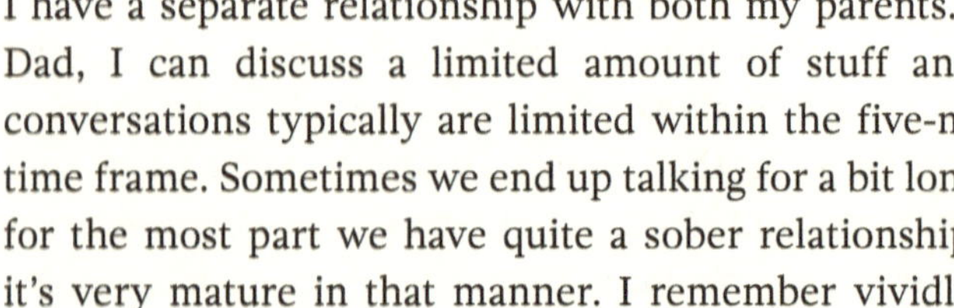

I have a separate relationship with both my parents. With Dad, I can discuss a limited amount of stuff and our conversations typically are limited within the five-minute time frame. Sometimes we end up talking for a bit long. But for the most part we have quite a sober relationship, and it's very mature in that manner. I remember vividly that I used to be very close to my father during my childhood and teenage years and suddenly one year this awkwardness crept in. I guess all boys go through this thing. We get closer to our mothers as we cross our adolescence, and we get farther away from our dads. In the recent years, I have been consciously trying to build a healthy relationship with my father. On the exact end of the spectrum, my conversations with Mom can easily cross threshold of an hour or two. We talk about movies, politics, religion, psychology and crack stupid jokes all the time. My younger brother Amaan, however, is the favourite child of my parents. I see him doing stuff that is worthy of a good threshing but both my parents just scold him and that's about it.

WTF?

I was whacked if I did something remotely naughty.

Hypocrisy?

My parents have been my support system since my childhood. They worked their asses off to provide me with the luxuries that they probably didn't receive in their childhood. I got admitted into the best school in the city. I wasn't a studious kid in school, but my parents motivated me to make the best use of my capabilities as a student. My mother and father both have been very supportive to me in terms of me choosing my own career path. Of course, we had our share of highs and lows as a family. But we emerged stronger every time.

The parent-child relationship is one that nurtures the physical, emotional and social development of the child. It is a unique bond that every child and parent feel simultaneously. This relationship lays the foundation of the child's personality, life choices and overall behaviour. It can also affect the strength of social, physical, mental and emotional health. Some of the benefits include-

- Young children who grow with a secure and healthy attachment to their parents stand a better chance of developing happy and content relationships with others in their lives.
- A child who has a secure relationship with his or her parents learns to regulate emotions under stress and in difficult situations.
- Promotes the child's mental, linguistic and emotional development.

In the end, I think we all realise that parents are also humans. They also feel the range of emotions just like us. Just because they are parents, we expect them to be perfect all the time. In this process, we forget an important aspect that they also get vulnerable, and they can also end up making mistakes. We can be wrong sometimes in analysing their situation. They are a couple and hence are bound to have arguments among themselves. Our father goes to office daily, works till evening, comes home by night. The least we can do as kids is to talk to him about his day and just joke around. Make him feel warm and happy. Our mothers in the same way give up on her personal life to provide us with all the necessities and luxuries that she probably didn't receive in her younger days. The lest we can do for the both of them is to appreciate their hard work and try to be nice to them. I have gotten into a bad fight with my parents many times. Sometimes it is about some mistake that I made whereas sometimes it is all just a big confusion. The best way to avoid conflicts with parents is to talk it out. We have been conditioned to believe as men that we can't be emotional and vulnerable but what's the truth in that. The same society that teaches us to be manly all the time, isn't around when we are hurt and want some emotional support. We are expected to be ready for challenges all the time. The big answer to all the confusion is to discuss the issue with your parents. Just because you are 21, doesn't mean you can't hug your mother or father. Just remain close to them, and you'll realise that nothing actually goes too wrong as long as your parents stay by you. Ending this paragraph with Karan Johar's favourite quote "It's all about loving your parents".

Taking turns to the concept of parenthood now.

"There are no bad children, just bad parents". The importance of parents in one's life is quite evident from this eminent quotation. Parenthood is a responsible venture and there's no debate on that topic. In this fast-paced era, it is quite difficult for parents to mark their presence in their children's life.

Millennial children who are exposed to distractions find it difficult to find a connection with the ordinary. Not to mention children are quite blinded by the reign of the virtual world. Child development lies its root in their parents. Nothing can overcome the rigidity of a child's upbringing. A parent thereby acts as a visionary to their children. Parents play a pivotal role in their children's life. They are the pillars of support, guidance, and love. Family is where life begins and love never ends. No matter how old a child gets, there's nothing more comforting and soothing than their parent's arms. The role of parents in a child's life is beyond the idea of prompting. Parenting takes action long before a child's birth and eventually parents become their children's alter ego and vice-versa. There is nobody like them who can shape and mould a child's behaviour and development. So parents should never seize to inspire and assist their children and thereby parents should strive to be the best teacher in their child's life.

Maintaining a good parent-child relationship is the first step towards wise parenting. Right from the birth of their offspring, parents should be aware of the enormous reliability and accountability in their child's life. Studies show that a fetus' character development is succumbed by the alterations in its mother's thoughts during pregnancy. Not giving the proper guidance and love can seriously affect a child's life and can have serious impacts that will lead to character defects. The parent is the child's first teacher and will remain a consistent mentor in a child's life. Parenting is a never-ending skill. Once you sign for it there's no looking back. You will have to take charge and make the most of your time. Parenting and child development are in a symbiotic relationship. When one flourishes, the other automatically finds balance. And this is the basic rule of every parent-child relationship. The profile of cognitive abilities, beliefs, ethical values, coping defenses, and salient emotional moods that characterise each child at each developmental stage is the result of diverse influences operating in complex ways.

Most students of human development agree that the most important determinants of the different profiles include the inherited physiologic patterns that are called temperamental qualities, parental practises and personality, quality of schools attended, relationships with peers, the ordinal position in the family, and, finally, the historical era in which late childhood and early adolescence are spent. As children develop from infants to teens to adults, they go through a series of developmental stages that are significant to all aspects of their personhood including physical, intellectual, emotional, and social. The proper role of the parent is to provide encouragement, support, and access to activities that enable the child to master key developmental tasks. A child's learning and socialisation are most influenced by their family since the family is the child's primary social group. Happy parents raise happy children. Child development lies its root in their parents. Nothing can overcome the rigidity of a child's upbringing. A parent thereby acts as a visionary to their children. There's nothing worldly that comes close to the sacrifices of parenthood. What parents do for their children out of love will always have an indelible remark on the child's life. A child who has never ceased to receive a balanced upbringing will continue to advance for the rest of their lives.

Education is one of the landmarks in a child's development. A good education will hand over a rewarding career to the person and thereby they can serve society and return its bounties. It is imperative to know how parents influence the lives of their offspring and play an important role in the child's physical, mental, financial, emotional, and career development. The importance of parents is something that children should comprehend involuntarily. It is not something that can be put forward as a moral or ethical question. Studies show that apart from earlier times, contemporary parents have a higher chance of failure to maintain a good relationship with their children despite the nuclear family setups that we have these days. Here is how you can build a successful rapport with your child-

- **Communication is the key:** Be it any relationship, communication is the foundation. Talk to your child about topics other than school and studies. This helps in contributing to better bondage between both parties.

- **Engage in activities with them:** You inevitably spend quality time with your loved ones. In this case, do something with your kid that is exciting for them. This will eventually help them polish their interests.
- **Apologise when you mess up:** Transparent and candidness can do wonders in your relationship. Throw away your ego and apologise for your mistakes. So that the child can stand up for themselves during future endeavours.

A recent study shows that parents who actively interact with children help them develop crucial cognitive skills, life skills, and eventually thrive to be successful. Parents contribute to developing focus, concentration, and self-control in their children. They also improve critical thinking, empathy, perspective, making connections, and communicating. With a supportive parent, a child never regrets taking risks and this prepares a self-directed child. Parents' interactions have a huge impact on the child's development, be it physical or mental. Apart from genetic inheritance, children have a tendency to mimic their parents in almost any field. This increases the liability of a parent to be a role model for their children. The efforts from a parent's side have great effects on their children. Even though each child is different and special in their capabilities, parents are the ones who can shape and assist their children without fail. It is the responsibility of parents to ensure a safe and sound environment for their children. "The attitude that you have as a parent is what your kids will learn from, more than what you tell them. They remember what you are"; these words by Jim Henson alarm us about the role of Parents in a child's life and justifies the impact and influence of parents in a child's life. Parenting is sometimes about finding happiness in sacrifices. And these sacrifices will not seize to rapture you in the long run. A child with a remarkable upbringing will never fail to make their parents proud. Parents are responsible to provide the necessary food, clothing, shelter, and medical care insofar as they are able.

They are equally responsible for providing sound education and sound knowledge of their religion as well as the moral training of their children. In the same way, children are responsible to appreciate their parent's promising efforts to ensure a good life for them. Having said all these, parenthood is not just about sacrifice, it is also teaching your child to master their life on their own. They should hand over responsibilities for their children so that they learn problem-solving skills at a young age. This will reduce the chances of being left out when they hit adulthood. So it's imperative that every parent decode their child's peculiarities and assist them in their overall development and thereby contributing to a better tomorrow. When a child is happy, then parents are happy. Parents do almost all the things to make their child educated and well respected in society. Whatever the situation or whatever is the problem that a child faces in life, parents should try and motivate and inspire them by their own examples to make a tough into good. Parents try to make the balance in their child's emotional persistence that helps to improve tough situations faster.

We as a family have gone through all phases of life, some positive and some negative. But that's the way of life. Quoting Mike Tyson "We never choose our family. We withstand them and grow up in a better world together".

It is the ultimate truth that not everyone is made for the perfect family life. For some individuals, maintaining a personal life is as necessary as maintaining a personal life. While for other people, the case might be completely different. Some people prefer to move out of their parent's place after getting married or finding a job. Whereas some people decide to stay with their parents and emerge as a family together. And no one is wrong in any regard, it all boils down to the choice that you as an individual are trying to make. I consider myself to be an individual of the second kind. I believe in the systematic way of living a family life. I've been living with them for the last 20 odd years and will continue to do so in the future as well.

As much as I like living with my parents, I am strongly against the idea of living with a joint family. I'm not referring to the grandparents and kids, I don't like the idea of leading life in the presence of aunts and uncles. I think they are not the kind of people that I would like to spend my time with. For readers' discretion, I'm mentioning this idea based on my experiences of living in a joint family. Not being a hater of the family system, I truly believe that a family staying in a joint system causes inconveniences and is the main reason for conflicts within the family. Obviously no two brothers or no two siblings in general will have the same level of success. One of them would obviously be earning more than the other one. Hence, feelings of envy settles down, and eventually the relationships get strained and the family breaks. The practical solution would be a family living in clusters, this would not only be helpful in the aspects of finance and economy but also in terms of the relationship growing and blossoming over time.

The idea of living in a family as much as it sounds all happy and happening, is pretty difficult. You have to make sure that everyone is on the same page. Sometimes what happens is that if two brothers are earning a sufficient amount of money, one of them backs off from the responsibilities in terms of the financial aspects while the other one remains adamant over his duties as a son. Over time, this relationship becomes strangled and eventually breaks up. The solution would be that both the brothers share an equal part of their incomes for the sake of taking care of their parents and all the other aspects of running a household. This is a progressive way of living that I would like to suggest to the millennial generation that includes me too. Some might not agree with me in this regard, but it's actually better to stay far away and happy than to live together in misery.

So, we come to the conclusion of the chapter. The one piece of information that one must imbibe from this piece of writing is that parents may not be perfect, they don't need to be perfect. No one is. Neither you nor me. Embrace their flaws and give them the love and respect they deserve. They had their bit of sleepless nights taking care of you. Now, it's your turn.

CHAPTER TWO

CHILDHOOD AND TEENAGE

"

Dare hue log aksar alfazon ke peeche chupte hai."

I watched the sun go down as I stood beside the Gomti river puffing on Classic Milds. Back home things had gone worse. Life was going on and on, but the void of peace had crept in. Fighting with a parent is not something I'm completely well versed with. My father had caught me smoking, and it turned out to be a bad phase in my life. Things were taking ugly turns now. Each day was getting screwed as the pile of taunts and soldering was getting into my head now. The sense of loneliness, depressive thoughts and just weird dark stuff was taking a toll on my mental health. All of it was very overwhelming and crazy at the same time. "What could go worse", I thought to myself. But the big guy in heaven stood watching my life getting embroiled with issues, day after day was enjoying the hell out of it.

This was a time during which I was reminiscing about my

childhood and all the fond memories I had of that time as they were the only thoughts that were offering me solace of any kind. The present was doom and remembering those happy moments of childhood was my only escape from the mundane reality. Childhood is probably the only time in one's life that a person enjoys himself or herself in the most innocent fashion. We don't have expectations from people, we live our hearts out without the fear of getting judged, we don't demand attention and just live to the fullest. We don't need to show our false identities to the cruel world. Things are simple and fun.

I grew up in an upper middle class Muslim household. My parents earned a decent amount of money and provided me with all the luxuries I could ask for as a child. Not bragging about my privileges, I celebrated my birthdays in the fanciest lounges and restaurants of the city growing up. I was given my own room at the age of seven. My mother bought me all the latest comics and video games. I have been a video game nerd since my childhood, so much so that I was the only boy in school who had the Nintendo Super Mario 2005 at the time of its release. I was also an avid fan of movies and going to theatres to watch a movie was a weekly event in my house. As already established in the first chapter that my parents run a school, I did my Montessori from the same school itself and got admitted into City Montessori School from kindergarten onwards.

A fun fact about my school, City Montessori School abbreviated as CMS is the largest school on Earth. It holds the Guinness Record of being the largest school in the world with more than 55 thousand pupils in the academic year 2016-17.

I did pretty well academically from kindergarten until class III rd. Class fourth was the time I got in the company of the kids the teachers referred to as the "Rowdy Boys". My mind changed its gears from studying to doing all sorts of nonsensical things. I went on from being the "Topper" to be the "class clown". My class teachers over the years referred to me as the "Worst of the lot". Very vividly I remember that every parent teacher meeting, my father used to stand in shame as my class teachers used to complain about my whereabouts to him.

On the topic of teachers, I would like to point out the fact that I really respect teachers because it's a hard job and a person literally spends much of his time teaching and educating his or her pupils. I think that I really enjoy being in the company of good teachers because my parents belong to the education business and hence I have an insight on what goes in the lives and minds of the teaching faculty. I have been raised in the company of teachers of my parent's school and have a cordial equation with them. My favorite teacher ever has been Ms Leena Chatterjee. She was my English teacher in the 11th and 12th standard. She was the teacher in my school life who didn't have any problems with my extrovert personality. Furthermore, she always motivated me to do my best. I was always a fan of the English Language growing up, and hence I struck a chord with all my English teachers while growing up. But Leena ma'am was the lady who ignited inside me the love for novels and most importantly Shakespeare. She was a role model in that regard. A well-spoken and cultured lady who carried herself with grace. She had a certain persona about her, her voice had a baritone and I always got intimidated by her presence. She always motivated me to make the best use of abilities as a student. I still remember she was the only teacher who believed that I could make it to the list of the meritorious students in the 12th board examinations. There are still a few more things regarding my childhood and teenage years that significantly shaped my character but also were the reason of huge struggles with myself and a great pain. When I was younger, I'd put my arms in my shirt and tell people I lost my arms. Would restart the video game whenever I knew I was going to lose. Slept with all the stuffed animals as a child so one of them felt offended. Had that one pen with 4 colours, and tried to push all the buttons at once. Poured soda into the cap and acted like I was taking shots. The hardest decision was choosing which Nintendo game to play. Waiting behind a door to scare someone, then leaving because they're taking too long to come out, or you had to pee. Faked being asleep, so I could be carried to bed. Used to think that the moon followed my car. Watching two drops of rain roll down the window and pretending it was a race. Went to the computer just to use Paint. I used to sing in the shower(Now? I make life decisions there now). Swallowed a fruit seed once, I was scared to death that a tree was going to grow in my stomach. Getting a bruised knee heals better than a broken heart. Remember when we were kids and couldn't wait to grow up. What the hell were we thinking?

I know firsthand that being a teenager is not always as easy as people say. While these years are often referred to as the best in one's life, the stress that comes with them is often overlooked. As if having to plan for your future is not scary enough, you are now old enough to uphold your own responsibilities. Some teens may have very few and are able to handle them lightly, while others take on many and find themselves struggling to keep up. Nonetheless, teenage years are still wonderful and should not be taken for granted. These are some of the lessons I have learned in my teenage life so far. I hope they will shine light on what being a young adult is like in this day and age. A Canadian statistics website called statcan.com states, "Many teenagers aged 15 to 19 have schedules just as busy as those of some adults." All teens have different activities consuming their time, but I will briefly describe some that I believe are the most significant. School is the most important responsibility in most teenagers' lives. Being in high school is almost equivalent to having a part-time job in some aspects. A significant portion of the day is spent in classes, and sometimes students can have up to hours in homework. A hardworking teen recognizes the importance of doing well in school and preparing for the future.

Peer Pressure is another issue a lot of teenagers face in the current scenario. Peer pressure has always been present and will also always be present. It is not a disease or a crime, it is an influence; either a negative or a positive one. Negative peer pressure is an influence put on a person to do something wrong, or something the person doesn't want to do. This may be stealing, taking drugs, or other dangerous actions. If someone influences you into doing something like this it is considered a negative peer pressure. This is a major problem in most schools all around the world. Teenagers usually feel peer pressure when they feel unpopular between their friends, or when they want to be accepted in a group of other teenagers. The group is a place where one feels accepted, where he can feel good about himself, where he feels secure. It increases his self-esteem, and it also enhances his self-image. Unfortunately, teenagers who want to be part of these groups, need to follow certain unpleasant routines which end up being fatal for their mental health.

One of the main aspects that parents neglect is the traumatic experiences a kid goes through in his childhood and teenage. Heinous acts like physical and sexual abuse that one faces in their childhood is not talked about much. Parents should focus on educating the children about this taboo topic a lot more. It is such a shame that most of these incidents occur in the family itself and the close family members are the ones who are usually responsible for something like this. A study done by UNICEF in 2018 shows that 81% of the child sexual abuse in the world is conducted by family members and close relatives. To understand the seriousness of this situation, I highly recommend watching the second episode of the first season of the Aamir Khan show "Satyamev Jayate".

In addition to that, I would also advise parents to subscribe to the notion of providing sex education to children at the starting of their teenage. A young teenager is the most fragile form of human species. This is the age during which a person goes through puberty and realises the physical changes in his or her body. They start getting attracted to people. And as a parent one should tell them that it's absolutely fine to feel so. Sex education would not only be informative for teenagers but also help them in understanding the physical aspects of the human body. Teenagers feel that they are not being heard, and their issues are not being addressed. They try to find the answers themselves and fall into traps. As a parent one should sit down with them and just answer their questions in the truest sense. A parent should talk about everything under the umbrella to his or her kids ranging from porn addiction and masturbation to periods and homosexuality. In my words, India has no right to call itself a progressive country until we open up our wooden conservative mindsets and break out to discuss these topics with our kids. There is a reason why the whole world looks up to the US. They were the first to legalise gay marriage. They were the first ones to talk about LGBTQ rights. As an upcoming economy, I feel that India should also change with times and make our thoughts more progressive and accepting.

For God's sake, we are the land of Kama Sutra and are the second most populous nation of the world and still consider talking about it a taboo.

Hypocrisy.

Hypocrisy.

Hypocrisy.

Be Aamir Khan from Taare Zameen Par not Alok Nath from Hum Saath Saath Hain.

"We are the generation of nostalgia. We grew up in the age of transition. From handwritten letters to electronic mails. From film to digital. We are fascinated by new things, neglecting the way we spend our afternoons. Cupcakes and tea. Play Tekken or Prince of Persia. Young and naive. Technology completely changed the way we waited and grew up too fast. The simple things in life seem more meaningful now. We grew up in the age of

transition and have become the generation of nostalgia. **"**

This is that time of one's life that a person feels to be correct all the time. The constant need for validation from parents, friends, family and society takes a toll on the psychology of the child. The fear of failure and the expectations to succeed completely disintegrates the charm of teenage and childhood. So much focus is laid on being the best that the inner innocence of being a teen is completely chucked out of the window. I am not trying to condemn the hard work one has to do in his teenage years to be successful in the future, I just want to point out that the constant need for validation will lead to nowhere. The only way out of the mess is to take one day at a time, chill, reflect and start it all over again.

Take wrong turns. Talk to strangers. Open unmarked doors. And if you see a group of people in a field, go find out what they are doing. Do things without always knowing how they'll turn out. You're curious and smart and bored, and all you see is the choice between working hard and slacking off. There are so many adventures that you miss because you're waiting to think of a plan. To find them, look for tiny interesting choices.

And remember that you are always making up the future as you go.

RELATIONSHIP & LOVE

"Baarishon mein bedhadak tere nachne se, baat baat pe bewajah tere roothne se, choti choti teri bachkani badmashiyon se, mohabbat karunga main ... jab tak hai jaan, jab tak hai jaan..."

Falling in love is the greatest feeling ever. This feeling that one individual feels towards the other is of the greatest value. The feeling that a parent has toward his or her child is insurmountable in the same way a husband loves his wife. This chapter however will be covering the romantic relationship that a person goes through in one's life.

For context, this is all from my perspective.

The butterflies that one gets in his stomach while asking a girl out for dinner.

A film date may be.

Or a Sunday brunch with cold coffee.

Sharing the headphones.

Waiting for them to call and being the one last to end it.

Passing the entire winter evening thinking of them.

Watching DDLJ and visualising them as the female lead.

Taking better care of your own health, so you can spend more years with her.

Fixing her hair when she has a bad hair day.

Making up in fights.

Open the door for her.

Taking long walks with her.

Sharing that last slice of that cheesy loaded pizza.

Massaging and calming her when she is on her periods.

Standing up and supporting her when she makes tough calls.

Letting her take her own decisions and just being behind her having her back if any stuff goes down.

Being a constant companion in her life.

Understanding her insecurities and helping her in overcoming them.

Making her proud of her imperfections.

Complementing not only her beauty but also her capabilities and presence of mind.

Just being there holding her hands.

That's what a lady wants.

To be loved.

And nothing else.

The perks of being in a relationship are innumerable. This one is going to take a while. Relationships of love haven't been my forte. I never understood the concept of falling in love ever.Let me lay it out more clearly.Relationships of love hadn't been my forte. I never understood the concept of falling in love ever.

Times are different now.

By the time I crossed the threshold of puberty, I had already become a porn addict. And as any self-proclaimed porn addict, I believed that to be the reality of life. I thought that love was all about the physical needs and jazz about intimacy. Something that was there just for the sake of it. But I always wondered whether I had any chance in striking a chord with someone. In the early 2010s, it was a fad in schools that ten-year-olds got into relationships. In hindsight, I think about that and wonder how immature and weird that is. Obviously this is something that I have learnt with time. But in those years even I wanted to be the chick magnet.

I was blessed with an extrovert personality and I loved talking to people ever since I was a teenager. But the moment it was about talking to someone of the other gender, I stood tongue-tied.

However, I tried to work around it and came to the conclusion that I was much more comfortable talking with girls when I used to channel the funny in me.

After completing my sixth grade I was promoted to seventh B(section). The first day, I laid my eyes on a girl who I instantly felt an attraction towards. This wasn't the first time I got turned on while seeing a girl. But it felt different. I went on to sit beside my best friend. Cut to, it's been two months since the summer vacations got over, as a rule of the class boys are made to sit with girls. Luckily I was made to sit next to her. In the coming weeks, we became good friends. I still remember she was always against the idea of keeping her backpack on the floor. We used to get in a lot of tussles over the same issue. Slowly we formed a cordial relationship in terms of friendship.

Every day, I went to school thinking of her on the way on a rickshaw, spending the entire day just blabbering with her about random stuff. We had lunch together every day. We played tic-tac-toe in the recess and every time there was a boring lecture. Furthermore, we became the best of buddies over time. I used to flirt with her in what I thought was the most innocent way.

Fast-forward, the annual term is over. She got very sick and couldn't give the final semester examinations and hence had to repeat the class. Meanwhile, I got into class eighth. Our friendship wasn't affected in this process at any stage. We still used to hang around in the recess. For readers' discretion, this was the time I was completely head over heels in love with her. I was hesitant to confess my feelings to her since she was not one of the girls who liked the whole girlfriend-boyfriend thing. She comes from a pretty conservative family.

This was the time I was watching my friends get into relationships and I thought to myself that if I don't express my feelings to her, I might lose her to a better looking guy in the near future. I gathered myself up and started planning on the prospects of wooing her. Finally, on 14th February (Valentine's Day), I decided that I'm just going to speak my heart out. I spent the entire school hours thinking of how I should say it to her.

What if she rejects?

What if she rejects and slaps?

What if she calls her father?

I gathered the courage somehow and made up my mind to just say it to her. We met in the campus playground after the school got over, and I confessed my feelings to her.

Sidenote- That proposal was cringed in retrospect.

She stood there in shock while I told her that she didn't have to reply at that moment, and she can take her time to do so.

The next day to my amazement, she replied in the affirmative. And that's how our story began. Obviously we had some rough patches in our relationship in the initial period, but we emerged as a strong couple over the course of the last decade. Currently, both of us are pursuing our respective undergraduate degrees. We have planned to get bonded into the holy bond of matrimony in the near future. The only regret I have is that I should have spent more time with her in the initial part of our relationship.

But letting bygones be bygones, we are in a much better and happy place now.

When tears fall from my eyes,
You were there to brush them away.
When I was lost in confusion,
You were there to say that everything would be okay.
When I stood before you falling apart,
You were there to lend your heart.
When I felt like no one would understand,
You were there to take my hand.
When no one was there to care,
You were there.

I have always been loyal to her and so has she. We have our fights and outbursts once a while, but I think that's what keeps the relationship hot and happening. The very fact that we can say our heart out to each other is the best thing of our relationship. We are honest with each other and call each other out on our shit. She is a religious girl and is quite adamant about it and despite being a super religious person she still believes in practicality and has an open mind unlike many orthodox religious people having a narrow mindset. I was never a religious person and didn't believe in a divine power and all those concepts. However, I have evolved over these ten years in terms of understanding my religion better. We have similar choices in many things. However, we have quite opposite tastes regarding some matters too. She likes things with a vintage touch while I'm all modern in that sense. She isn't a foodie like me. She likes winters and I hate them. However, we are completely fine with each other's likes and dislikes.

Being in love means acceptance.

Acceptance of each other's qualities and flaws.

Acceptance of the fact that it is not always going to work your way.

Acceptance that your partner will screw up.

Acceptance that you will screw up.

But acceptance of the fact that the love which bloomed between you two in the first place will remain unchanged.

Most of the people believe that being in a relationship is all about the physical intimacy and all that kinky sex. However, that is of no use if the relationship doesn't have love in it. The best part in my humble opinion of getting in a relationship is the emotional support an individual receives from the other person. When you are at your lowest, your partners will be present for you, and you'll be there when they are in the same level of misery and insanity.

Not being sexist and saying that all girls are shopaholics, I would humbly add that my one is quite a shopper. She has a very classy and elegant taste in things while I'm the louder one. She doesn't like my fashion sense and constantly tries to mould me. However, it doesn't imply that she is controlling. She likes me to make my own decisions, however she advises me when I'm in a bad place or whenever I'm not clear enough to make the right calls.

She is the best.

She is awesome.

She is lit.

She is my best friend.

She is my companion.

She is my support.

We have changed over the last ten years and I can firmly say that our relationship has evolved in this decade, and we are in a happy place now.

Ten years?

Time flies.

Few more years of grind, and we'll be together for eternity.

~

I don't think you will
 Ever fully understand
 How you've touched my life
 And made me who I am.
 I don't think you could ever know
 Just how truly special you are,
 That even on the darkest nights,
 You are my brightest star.
 You've allowed me to experience
 Something very hard to find,
 Unconditional love that exists
 In my body, soul and mind.

I don't think you could even feel
All the love I have to give,
And I'm sure you'll never realise
You've been my will to live.
You are an amazing person,
And without you, I don't know what I'd be,
Having you in my life
Completes and fulfils every part of me.
I know the sheer amount of poetry in this chapter is completely overbearing,
But I could not think of any other way of displaying my love and caring.

I wanted to end this chapter now as it has already become very mushy. But I'm compelled to write a few paragraphs more talking about certain serious issues.

I have never gone through a break-up or separation.

Thank God for that.

Hence, I don't have anything to add to that conversation from my end. But over the years, I've seen many of my close friends and colleagues separating from their respective partners. I acknowledge that it is a dark place to be, and it's easier said than done to just move on. Breakup or divorce or any kind of heartbreak can be fatal to the emotional health of a person.

People who aren't in relationships feel that it is very easy to just bury the past and continue with life. However, I firmly believe that it's okay to not be over someone for some time. You can reflect on your thoughts and take your time to lament for your loss. It's absolutely fine.

The one solution that I can come up with is to keep yourself busy in the things and activities that you enjoy.

Activities that make you happy. Sit and chill with friends who have your best interest at mind.

Maybe have a vacation.

Or a long drive.

Have a cheat day.

Binge-watch that old guilty film that you have hots for.

Work on yourself.

Keep yourself sane, and you'll soon realise that it is not all gloomy.

Do whatever it takes to fill that void. Chat with your parents and share your worries with them, and you'll find out that there is light at the end of each dark tunnel.

However, accept the fact that it is over and keep yourself in a stable position. Stay away from the idea of rebound because it will never be the same again, and it will all lead to pain in the end.

No reason.

I'll say that again, no reason is big enough to end your life after.

Suicide is not the way.

Self-harm is not the way.

If you are suffering mentally consider going to a therapist. Going to a therapist can turn out to be a boon and very soon you'll realise that you're not the villain of your life. Your mind will get clear, and you will finally be able to move on with your life. Seeking medical help is not shameful. You are doing it for yourself. Don't let the society and people around you tell you otherwise. They are not going through the trauma, you are.

Getting sad thoughts and feeling miserable during the initial period of a breakup is completely normal. The most adequate solution is to talk about it. I don't know why our society considers it a taboo when an individual wants to talk about his or her failures, which also includes heartbreak. Living in a toxic relationship is considered advisable instead of ending it and being in a happy and satisfied place in life. The only person that you must listen to at this time is yourself.

Go through the dark phase, and you'll emerge out strong and victorious.

That brings us to the end of this chapter, JUST ONE LAST PIECE OF POETRY-

Many things can make me happy,
many things can make me smile,
many things can make life wonderful,
make it all seem so worthwhile.
But nothing makes me happier than the special friend
I've found.
Life couldn't feel more stunning when you're around.
In the short time since I met you, I've soon come to
know how special you are to me, much more than you
know.
Whenever we're together, my life feels so complete.
I feel so blessed that we got the chance to meet.
You really are so beautiful; your life could light the
dark,
Your touch and your soft embrace bring such warmth
to my heart.
I'd cherish you 'til the end of time and always be there
for you.
I'd care for and protect you, and I'd never let you down.
I'd be your rock at those times when you need someone
around.
I'd stand by you through bad times and keep you safe
from harm.

I'd be your guardian angel, and you'd be my good luck
charm.
Life would be great adventure with you there by my
side,
building memories of happiness as I hold your hand
with pride.
And as time slowly slips away, and we're growing old
with grace,
I'd still adore you just as much as when I saw your face.
If this seems like a crazy dream,
well may be that is true,
but my dream became reality the day I met you.

CHAPTER FOUR

BEING A MUSLIM AND VIEWS ON RELIGION

"*Mann se Raavan jo nikale,*
Ram uske mann mein hai."

DISCLAIMER

The following chapter that you are about to read dwells on my thoughts on religion, and hence readers' discretion is highly advised.

The chapter or the author(me) does not intend to offend the feelings/sentiments of any individual, caste, creed, community, race or religion or denigrate any person/profession/trade/institution whether living or dead.

I will try my best to keep this chapter completely unbiased and free of any controversial elements that could possibly make me end up behind bars.

Now that it has been stated, let's start the chapter.

Hinduism and Islam are the major religions followed in our nation. Not being condescending in acknowledging the existence of several other religions, I will talk about my religion, which is Islam, if that's not apparent from my name.

So, will this chapter be another piece of writing that will hurt people's religious sentiments?

No.

'No' is a strong term; let me say that it depends on your perspective and how you look at things.

I'll try to be sensitive in regards to the choice of my words. Let's start by addressing the elephant in the room—Religious sentiments.

What are they? What is the chemical composition of religious sentiments?

And how weak are your sentiments that they get hurt by a joke made by a stand-up comedian or a piece of writing.

Hoping that I won't land up in any sort of legal trouble for saying this, I must state that we as a nation are religious-phobic. I don't know if that's a term. When I say religious-phobic, I mean that the majority of people in our beautiful country are condescending to other religions except their own. Spreading hate and promoting violent attacks is not what God desires. At least I hope not.

For centuries now, we have divided people on the basis of their religion, which essentially boils down to the fact whether you consume red meat or not. I am too scared to even mention the name of the animal as the mere mention can cause havoc in my simple life. One section likes breaking religious places of worship while the other one continues to yell at loudspeakers five times a day. Why can't the two coexist peacefully?

Is our country intolerable? No. Hell no.

Can it become intolerant in the future? Probably yes.

I'm going to talk about Islam in this chapter as this was the religion I was born into. My parents are Muslims and hence it seems like a smooth and logical progression to be identified as a Muslim.

I believe that everyone knows what a Muslim is?

Yes, you guessed it right, we are the creatures that walk into mosques on Fridays.

Our women wear the batman outfit over their normal clothes while stepping out of the house.

We have 4 wives and 12 kids.

We get married to our sisters.

We don't take a bath.

We don't stand up for the national anthem.

Our favorite colour is green.

Our favourite date is 9/11.

We are huge on TikTok (we were huge on TikTok).

We produce fast bowlers in cricket.

We worship a faceless God.

We hate our prime minister for some reason.

We send our family members to middle eastern countries to earn their livelihood because it's tax free and a large amount of money is required to feed a family of 25.

We eat beef, cook beef, and sell beef. We own tunday kababi. No one hates tunday; even Hindus love it, despite the fact that it is prepared in a Muslim kitchen.

These are some of the stereotypes that Muslims are subjected to in the society and some of them are probably true but we are trying to better ourselves, at least I am.

Indulging in a bit more on this now.

Muslims or musalmans as many may say, have been residing in India since the early phase of the Delhi sultanate. And like all people, some of our forefathers and ancestors have done some questionable stuff in the past. Be it Mahmud Ghaznavi or Aurangzeb, as much as they are allured by our community, we should realise that they weren't necessarily the nicest people. The Mughal Empire as a whole was not great either. Breaking temples to build mosques is not something that the Almighty Allah wants. Killing innocents in the name of 'jihad' is not done.

I agree that some people from our community have done some bad shit in the past and we should never forget that. But I think in all fairness that Muslims today should not bear the brunt of some terrible thing that a ruler did in the 17th century AD.

I hear people say sometimes- Why did you break the Ram mandir? I'm like, "Bro, what the hell are you talking about. I'm here, stuck in my mundane life, not being able to break the monotony, and you're asking me about why I broke the temple". Babur did it, not me. Don't blame that shit on me. He is not my family relative either, whom I would just randomly drunk dial and order to break a whole place of worship down. I hope I'll meet him in the afterlife and offer him a chilled tuborg can and probably listen to his end of the story.

Well, I was brought up in a pretty conservative family. Questioning the very religion that we follow would end up in a well-choreographed walking session by my family members and hence I always stayed away from the idea of applying any logic to religion in general. Growing up, I was a crazy fan of movies and got this sense that Muslims are portrayed in a bad light in pop culture. Grew up and realised the reason. The sheer incompetence on the part of some individuals from our community made me believe that there is a reason as to why we are the most misunderstood religion in the world. I heard the word 'Jihad' for the first time while watching My Name is Khan.

'Jihad' literally means 'struggling' or 'striving'. That's the literal translation. Context is required for understanding any concept in religion. 'Jihad' has two different meanings according to the Quran, one is 'greater jihad' which means jihad which a person goes through with his or her inner demons to become a better individual and the other is 'lesser jihad' which means the jihad one does for his people.

This term was coined by Prophet Muhammad as a means to give the people a way to look around themselves and better the place and eventually themselves. However, with the US invasion of Islamic nations, the concept of 'jihad' has got an all together different meaning. A person of any terrorist organization is now referred to as a 'jihadi'. We as a community have forgotten the real meaning of jihad. Jihad means to fight your inner insecurities, jihad means to protect your people, your nation and the world. Killing millions of innocent people across the globe is not jihad. I consulted various Islamic texts, and none of them claims that jihad needs to be violent in any kind. Weapons should only be picked up if your 'watan' (nation) is in danger, that's the only exception according to the various texts.

The word 'jihad' is mentioned in the Quran about 41 times, while the words 'peace', 'mercy' and 'compassion' are mentioned 355 times. Contrary to the belief in most western cultures, Islam is a religion that preaches peace and tolerance. Now that's lead us to a question- If Islam truly is a religion that preaches peace then how come the world's most troubled spots be it the West Bank, Afghanistan, Pakistan or Iraq are plagued with Islamic terrorism? Answer - That's depend on your definition of terrorism. Some might argue that the US invasion of countries like Iraq and Afghanistan for their petroleum reserves were also acts of terrorism. People think that those were the acts of war to get rid of despotic regimes, however they were the means of getting a country's oil. Taliban was a creation of the CIA to fight the Russians and America's very own intelligence agency has admitted to it.

Most of the Muslims around the world are unaware of Islam in its purity. They don't read the Quran or the other related texts and follow so-called maulanas and maulvis who are the ones truly responsible for the deteriorating condition of Muslims across the world. Seldom do people actually recite the Quran with translation and hence they turn towards these god-men for understanding the meaning of the verses, and it's here that they fool us. The Quran is a very layered and subjective book. Even a slight change in the pronunciation can completely change the meaning of the verses.

Understanding your religion by yourself is sufficient. I think that worshipping God/Allah/Bhagwan is enough, we don't need to worship these god-men to attain nirvana or jannat(in case of Muslims). Most of the god-men around us have been extremely fatal, be it Asaram Bapu, Zakir Nayak or MSG. Our relationship with god-men is very similar to that of Kabir Singh with Preeti, he abuses us, and we eventually come back to him, and who wants to be in a toxic relationship?

Muslims in our country have a very narrow mindset. Not generalizing, but that's the truth. Even some woke

Muslims might agree. We think that religious teaching is the only way a person can survive. I do agree that for each person his or her religion is of utmost importance and there's no two ways about it, but living life with practicality is what should be prioritized. The thousand-year-old traditions which are outdated and problematic should be dusted into the bin of the past. We as a community should seriously consider education as a very important aspect in a person's overall development. Indian Muslims have the lowest literacy rate across Muslims around the world. And that's the bitter truth. We should accept that and move on to bring glory to our community, which would eventually help in building a better India. If we as a community start realizing the true meaning of Islam, and become more aware and be civil and educate ourselves, then there's still hope for us, otherwise it's all downhill from here. I know that this piece of writing up till now will not get me into any trouble, as it's written in English and ....

Is religion becoming problematic?

Nope,

But the orthodoxies are at it.

Why would a man just appointed to the position of Chief Minister of a state, with the huge job of improving the lives of its citizens on his hands, begin his innings by commenting on what appears to be his foremost concern- 'Women wearing ripped jeans'?

What idea of religion or spirituality could possibly inspire a true believer to brutally beat up a child who came to a place of worship to drink water, merely because of the community the child belonged to? And who are the people who are still trying to find excuses and justifications for such execrable, inhuman behaviour.

Like conservatives in Afghanistan who are aghast at the idea of women singing, or of those in Iran who abhor the idea of a woman being out with a man not her relative, or those in Saudi Arabia who cannot countenance the notion of ladies keeping their heads and faces uncovered, they are determined to preserve what remains of the social order they believe is moral.

So, when it comes to the fact that we as Indians take great pride in our history and culture, we should remember the atrocities herald upon women and those of low castes throughout history. History is always written with an intent to glorify the past, not the reality that people faced during that era.

Yes, we are a great nation. NOW.

Have we been a great nation this whole time? QUESTIONABLE.

Whatever progress societies around the world have achieved is in spite of such elements, not because of them. The orthodox Hindus in India 200 years ago fought to preserve the practice of sati or burning widows at the funeral pyres of their husbands, which was outlawed by Bengal Sati Regulation of 1829. When they failed at this, they battled against widow remarriage, against the likes of Ishwar Chandra Vidyasagar. In subsequent years, they did not want girls and those of lower castes to be educated. They also did not want people of lower castes to even walk on the same roads as them, or to wear proper clothes. In Kerala, it took a movement to 'allow' women of lower castes to cover their breasts because there was a 'breast tax' on low caste women wearing clothes on their upper bodies.

Orthodox Muslims have been no better in this regard. Some of the regressive practises that took birth thousands of years ago are still very much in play. They get proud of the fact that women are kept in confinements. Forcing them to wear burqa or hijab is something that has been prevalent for centuries now. It's not about the girl's choice. We decide what's good or bad for her. We will burn her if she falls in love with a guy from a different religion. And then we have the audacity to take pride in our beliefs.

The old elites everywhere in India certainly did not want women and lower castes to compete for the same jobs as upper caste men. At every step, their stupid, obdurate resistance was overcome by the progressives and liberals of those times and places. It helped that a British colonial government was in power, because if the local elites had been in power, such social transformation would not have been possible. That's probably the only time the British did something which was better for us.

We are now seeing what it is like when political as well as social power are concentrated in the hands of the kind of people who rigidly defend ancient traditions of discrimination. Indeed, they want to bring back their "golden age", one where women and lower castes were treated worse than cattle.

Small minds and hearts cannot conceive of any cause greater than the sum of their prejudices.

I'm neither targeting Hinduism nor Islam here. I'm just showing the bigotry that goes both ways in the mindsets of the orthodoxies. People who think that they are the ones who will save their religion from the possible threat are the ones who actually end up being the threat. Love Jihad and mob lynching is done by those having an orthodox mindset. It's the mindset which makes the entire difference. No one wants to be accepting of the other's faith, and thus we fail as humanity all together.

On the bright side, I have seen things changing over the past decade or so. But the velocity of this change needs to accelerate and not stop to make our nation a better place. People should really consider the idea of living with principles that aren't sexist, misogynistic or problematic. And that's the solution which humanity needs.

Ending this chapter with a poem I wrote back in Xth standard. It goes like:

I asked for wisdom...

And God gave me

problems to solve.

I asked for prosperity...

And God gave me brains

and the strength to work.

I asked for courage...

And God gave me danger

to overcome.

I asked for love...

And God gave me

troubled people to help.

I asked for favours...

And God gave me

opportunities.

I received nothing, I

wanted.

I received everything I

needed.

My prayer has been

answered.

CHAPTER FIVE

NEWS AND OPINIONS

"

Jahan lakshya hona chahiye tha khabarein aur madhyam hona chahiye tha paisa, wahan aaj paisa ban gaya hai lakshya, aur khabarein keval madhayam."

Before indulging in, let's address some of our favourite Indian news channels-

To Republic TV,

Hey man, you do know that we are not watching you for the news.

Right? You do know that.

We don't watch you for the news, we just like watching your prime anchor shouting at the top of his lungs, "The nation wants to know", or another one going, "Deepika ki gaadi, Deepika ki gaadi".

We are watching Republic TV for the same reason we watch Bigg Boss.

The only difference between you and the Bigg Boss is that the people in the Bigg Boss house are already locked up, and you soon will be.

To NDTV,

When are you going to realise that you don't have the moral high ground?

You are not better than anybody else.

The people on your panels are so excited by the sound of their own voice.

It's like watching people pleasure themselves to their own words.

The only people who watch your panels are the people on those panels.

Can you please give us the news in a way that the common citizens understand?

To ZEE News,

Can you just stick to serials and daily soaps?

If you are using the same background music for the financial budget or breaking news as you are for that moment where Kumkum drops the pooja ki thali, you are not a news channel any more.

To INDIA Today,

Who are you?

Literally, what do you represent apart from successful advertising revenue?

You channel flip-flops more than the chappals that we throw at politicians' faces.

Maybe that's why we call you INDIA Today because you don't know what you're going to be tomorrow.

You are not an establishment, rather an anti-establishment.

All you are is intermittent ads for Lovely Professional University.

Headlines such as "Maut ka Bathtub" at Sridevi's death, "Kya aliens peete hai gai ka doodh" during beef ban etc remind us of how low our Indian news channels have stepped down where a cheeky and clickbait headline matters more than the actual news itself.

Oh, Man!

Here's a thing that I've learnt from watching Indian news channels for years now. Everything you read and watch in the news is not necessarily the truth.

Right?

Here's how the news in India boils down.

Just a reminder. I'm not commenting or targeting any particular Indian news channel, as all of them are at the same level of misery.

News follows views. It is no longer about the truth. The truth is extremely complicated and nuanced, and the news is meant to be sexy and fast. The truth takes a long time to understand. However, the media and news channels don't have that amount of time to brainstorm over the topics of discussions and give an unbiased take. That is why news channels usually have sections like '70 news in 7 minutes' etc. It's no longer about giving the context regarding the news, it's about the number of viewers that you can get to watch that section.

For example, if we take the Kashmir issue. If someone comes and says, "Hey, tell me about Kashmir". You are like, "Okay, here's what I've read about Kashmir. Let's go back seventy years ago, when India as a country was being formed after independence". In this case, the person is more likely to be agitated. He'll be like, "I want to know the current thing. Why have you gone seventy years back". But if you want to understand something in depth, it requires context, which the news doesn't have space for. Unfortunately, the news channels want to put up the news in a sensual way and get all the eyeballs to be at the top of the TRP game.

I would suggest for more people to stop looking for news as the absolute truth. Start using your brains instead. First, don't consume every piece of news that you see. Watching each piece of news makes people start judging other people and thinking that everyone is either black or white and there's no grey. The gospel truth however is the fact that everybody is grey. No one is completely true and no one is completely false. We are all just partially informed people who think that our opinion is correct and millions of other people's opinions stand wrong in front of our own biases. We are ready to get angry at people without thinking for a second if the person has even a slightly different opinion from ours. The constant need to see things go your own way often leads one to a gloomy place. I think the Internet fundamentally changed the day retweets were invented, the day there were like buttons and comment sections on YouTube and Instagram because it started to give people an incentive to behave in a way that could get them likes and not react genuinely to anything.

For example, if Kangana Ranaut or Karan Johar tweet something, and it makes sense, then also a certain group of people are present to boycott them because they are either uninformed or they don't know the context or simply cannot fathom the fact that someone has an opposite opinion which doesn't suit their narratives or biases.

And the worst thing about the news that I just don't understand is the debates on the panels. First, you get the least qualified people to be on these debates. I think that the news channels do so, so that they can have a stand-up comedy show for a duration of an hour, as most of the time the people on these panels discuss which comedian to boycott. It can range from Tanmay Bhat's Snapchat story scandal to AIB roast and the recently controversial Vir Das's two India speech at the Kennedy Centre. Second, the pathetic lust to ban movies. Some of which include Hansal Mehta's directorial Aligarh, Aamir Khan's PK or SRK's My Name is Khan. However, the winner in this case is Sanjay Leela Bhansali, I mean wow. All of his movies ranging from Devads, Ramleela, Bajirao Mastani and Padmavat(i) have been discussed on the news panels. Third, the ever longing desire to be at the top of the rating list. Ever wondered how each of the news channels that we have in our nation quote themselves as the "Number 1 news channel in India".

Some of my favourite Indian news channel debates over the years-

- <u>The Demonetization Debate</u>- A certain Hindi news channel got a panellist from the current ruling party, and the way he supported the government's decision was illogical and hilarious at the same time. I loved how he said that the two thousand rupee note had a chip (a GPS tracker) which would track the black money. He also slapped a woman panellist on the same debate for having a differing opinion and guess what, he got a vidhayak ticket form the political party that very month. I have nothing left to say.

- <u>AIB Roast Controversy</u>- AIB (I won't mention the full form as the publishers might cancel me) along with many A list Bollywood actors held a knockout roast at the Jio Garden in Mumbai. Legal charges were pressed as usual because that is what we do. Now, we as people thought that the judiciary would make a decision regarding the matter. Nope. The news channels saw it as a perfect opportunity to make some headlines. A certain English News Channel brought up a debate headlined as "Is comedy meant to be offensive?". The debate went on for a long two-hour session and many horrendous remarks were made by both the individuals supporting the notion and the ones opposing it. One such man present at the debate was a stand-up comic who has clearly been past his prime, his name is Sunil Pal. He said and these are his exact words, "Aajkal ke comedy shows mein sirf gay log aur chakke aate hai, agar aisi audience hogi to stand-up comedy ka sthar girega, zahir si baat hai". His comment is very problematic. Firstly, he is being a homophobic person and shameful towards the LGBTQ community. Secondly, he is speaking in Hindi at an English news debate. It only shows us that some people are ready to be a**holes just to gather some limelight and stay relevant

- <u>International Yoga Day</u>- This debate dates back to 2018 when a live debate was held on Aaj Tak. Baba Ramdev is a yoga enthusiast, as we all know, and he is surely very good at that. So much so that when a panellist asked him about the benefits of yoga, he stated that yoga can cure homosexuality. I agree that yoga is beneficial for the body, but I seriously cannot get over the fact that a yoga guru can say such things. Yoga does a lot of things, but I don't think that it can change your sexual preferences. A man of his stature and influence should think before saying something which is so out of logic and bizarre.

These are just a few of them which caught my attention. I now know why we don't have good TV shows in our country because the best fiction writers work in the news.

Indian media today is trapped by power centres, business tycoons and Indian state authorities converting their role of watchdog to lapdog, to which critics in India characterise as 'godi' media. Deteriorating the fundamental principles of journalism and ethical standards would cost the Indian media industry and the academia a lot of bringing back the credibility that is taught in universities and institutes across India. Much time is being spent critiquing the individual anchors and lamenting their partisan coverage on news. But perhaps they are merely a manifestation of a deeper malaise that has gripped the entire system. By removing one anchor or fining one particular news channel, this malaise will not go away. It is a global virus and has been playing out almost similarly in other parts of the world. It's at the same level in first world countries as well. Hence, I want to recommend the people who read the news and judge people to not do that as it is unhealthy for you, and it makes your sense of judgement impaired, and your perspective too gets muddled.

Watching Indian news channels has now become a national sport of entertainment. In terms of what is going on with the media in general and how they operate, many channels are becoming like an ad running for the government. In 2014 just after the Lok Sabha elections, we as citizens saw the biggest shift in our news channels. The very news channels which were whitewashing the Congress's image turned against them and the ones questioning BJP became it's biggest supporters. In September 2015, there was a scuffle between the US and Pakistan, all the news channels across the world reported it and went ahead. Meanwhile, the Republic TV in Mumbai goes, "Is this victory for the Modi Government?".

I mean what. How does a conflict between two nations become a victory for a third nation?

These news channels now will just link anything with everything and create something that will result in absolutely nothing.

These news channels don't realise that the government will get praise for doing good work and if the government is doing it then there's no need for them to spew out the propaganda. And if pleasing the government is that important for these channels, why don't they ask the Prime Minister of India to address a press conference?

By the way, I'm still waiting for my fifteen lakhs. Maggi Ji, it's time for 'dhan ki baat'.

Jokes aside, is there really an answer for the hot question-Why has the level of Indian journalism gone so low?

The media in India has grown into an economic giant, with a business turnover which exceeds one percent of the country's gross domestic product (GDP) and matches the economic size of many individual industries in India.

However, even with such growth, somehow the level of journalism has just gone down. The media in India has played a disproportionate role in shaping public perceptions of politics, electoral outcomes and the way power is exercised. Media personalities (news anchors, journalists etc) rub shoulders with top-level politicians, industrialists and corporate lobbyists and collude in making key government appointments and influencing policy decisions. In sharp contrast to the immense financial power and political clout of the Indian media stands its indifferent and generally declining - quality, reliability and authenticity, loss of diversity, and pluralism, shallowness in reporting and comment on serious issues, and systematic violation of elementary norms of responsible journalism. The latest example of the incompetence of Indian journalism is the Aaryan Khan drug controversy. Facts are getting sidelined and things are being taken out of context. And this is not the first time that things are taken out of context, it's always the case with our media and news channels.

In recent years, the Indian media has lowered the quality of India's public disclosure. Media expansion has led to a shrinking of the public sphere, and spread of elitist and socially retrograde values. This is producing a growing and potentially grave crisis of credibility. The low and falling quality of Indian journalism is evident in a number of ways-

- First, this country of 1.2 billion cannot claim to have a single magazine of ideas or literary journal of international standards. In my humble opinion. Nor does it publish a significant number of influential newspapers which are independent of corporate cartels. There is very little diversity in the range of social and political views expressed in the mainstream media.

- Second, the media no longer adequately performs the primary functions it is meant to, which give it public legitimacy - namely, informing the people, telling the truth, analysing complex social, economic and political processes, providing a platform for public debate and acting as the people's watchdog or conscience.
- Third, the newspapers which are in circulation today contain less news and more advertisements. In my humble opinion, 'The Hindu' is the only newspaper which thinks otherwise. There is a reason why all the UPSC aspirants go through 'The Hindu' for their daily dose of current affairs and news all around the world. This is not a placement or a plug. This is just honest customer feedback.
- Fourth, despite rapid globalisation and the opening up of Indian society and culture to international influences, the Indian media remains extremely insular. There is remarkably paltry coverage of international issues, events, institutions and processes

This is, admittedly, a pretty darning list of flaws. But no less disturbing are; editorializing in the news pages; heavy slanting of headlines and photo captions; censorship of views critical of ruling orthodoxies and of stories written from the standpoint of the underprivileged and the vulnerable; and blacking out of the coverage of unconventional, radical or non-mainstream movements and organisations (including campaigns for peace, human rights, global justice, or sexual equality).

Even more unconscionable is the blatantly partisan support in large sections of the media for a particular political party, marginalisation of readers' or viewers' opinion, and a systematic refusal to admit and correct errors of fact.

The media, as it exists and is evolving today, is simply not designed or meant to report on the existing reality of Indian society or inform the public on the economic and political processes at work in it, including shifts in social values and in the balance of power between different groups, and new forms of political competition—leave alone promote a comprehension of the complex social dynamics that are shaping decision-making structures and India's changing relations with the rest of the world.

Perhaps the most telling comment on the Indian media lies not in the stories it has done, but in the stories it has missed or killed.

To be fair, it is not that the media never carried these stories. It did—reluctantly, belatedly, half-heartedly, sloppily, following many entreaties by the concerned investigators, or after the issue had already figured in the national or state legislature. It did not originate from them, as it should have. These important facts, which speak of dysfunctions in the deepest interstices of Indian society, were unearthed, noted, discovered, compiled, collated and disseminated by others.

The mainstream journalistic paradigm in the Indian print media (with a few honourable exceptions) is shockingly insensitive to the real concerns of flesh-and-blood people, especially the vast majority of Indians who are poor and underprivileged. Its principal—and matter-of-factly stated—aim is to promote the "feel-good" factor and "pump sunshine" into the life of the consumerist elite.

Headlines in most papers show strong biases: e.g. telecom is "liberated" (i.e. recklessly privatised, with harmful consequences, as in the 2G scam), and imports of

1,400 items are "freed" (to promote unregulated imports which could ruin millions of farmers).

What takes the cake is the memorable headline: "India, Beauty Superpower of the world, wins the Miss Universe crown". This is when Indian women have worse malnutrition levels than women in sub-Saharan Africa—after two decades of agrarian distress, economic collapse, ethnic conflict, civil war and famine in that continent. What matters is not the truth, but the "feel-good" factor, the daily dose of steroids the Indian elite so desperately needs—and gets—through the media.

These trends highlight the Indian media's increasingly conservative and retrograde character in a period which demands a radical review of conservative approaches, and exploration and examination of alternative options to policies that are failing, ideologies that are proving bankrupt, and mindsets that are patently sterile.

The Indian media now faces a serious crisis of credibility. If it does not reform itself, it will find its greatest asset getting rapidly devalued and eventually vanishing. Robbed of authenticity, reliability and credibility, the media will cease to matter to large numbers of people except as a source of cheap entertainment and titillation. Journalism will then cease to be all that makes it worthy and socially relevant: an honest, investigative, analytical, public-oriented and ethical pursuit.

That would be a grave tragedy and a terrible disservice both to democracy and to the causes of enlightening and empowering the public.

The only way to get the Indian news channels and media report in an ethical way is to stop consuming it. When the media world realises that they aren't getting enough eyeballs, the content itself will start getting better.

No matter who you are, everyone has the right to have their opinions. The opinions may be political, social or religious. And it's not wrong to have a contrary opinion as compared to the majority. Unfortunately, we as a country are living in a land where you can either be a supporter of the government or a hater. Nobody wants the lines to get blurred. No one realises that you can be a rational being who applies his or her brain and form your personal opinion. You are considered a rightist if you support the government once, and are immediately tagged as a leftist if you speak against the government. Unfortunately, there is no middle ground. I have never been a fan of labels, and this is the time and age where everyone is getting labelled. If you stand with Narendra Modi regarding some of his policies you are immediately labelled a "bhakt" whereas if you criticise any of his decisions you are advised to go to Pakistan. I think there is a lot of grey area left unnoticed. People cannot fathom the fact that the same person can criticise the government as well as appreciate it.

For example, I never understood the concept of demonetization. For people living under a rock, PM Shri Narendra Modi in 2016 announced that all the currency notes of the denomination of five hundred and one thousand will not remain valid any more. This decision was taken by the central government to curb black money and eventually raise the degrading economy of the nation. I never saw the whole point of this activity. Hence, it is my personal opinion that demonetization was a futile exercise. I may be false or I may be true. It doesn't mean that demonetization was a bad thing. It might be simply the case that I'm uninformed or that I'm not well versed with the technicalities behind the complete thing. On the other hand, I wholeheartedly supported the decision of introducing GST as it made the lives of tax paying citizens simpler. GST brought the unified taxation system and people were saved from the random taxes that each state charges. The system of division of taxes into four slabs was something that many supported. It doesn't make me a bhakt or rightist, for that matter. In both these situations, my objective remained the same, to see my nation's progress. However, one policy was considered extraordinary by me, whereas the other one was simply a waste. And this is what a citizen should do. Let the things play out and see for yourself and make the decision.

Another point that I would like to add to this conversation is that usually people vote for a certain party not for the merit of the party but for religious reasons. It is understood that if you are a Muslim you can never vote for the BJP, if you are from any scheduled caste your preferred party is BSP and if you are a liberal you will vote for the Congress. It is a notion that needs to be modified. We should vote for the country and choose a leader not because he favours a particular section but thinks about building the country as a whole. Our nation has good politicians, but we are devoid of good political leaders. The difference between the two seems very subtle but is actually very broad. Politicians want to win the elections and come to power, while political leaders enter the field for the betterment of the nation. Politicians take our nation to the dogs while political leaders take it to the heights.

So, is it okay to have a different opinion?

The answer is Yes. Absolutely.

Having an opinion, particularly one that other people don't like, means that your brain is active, and you have the ability to think. These opinions could simply be thoughts or may be the result of logical or of scientific reasoning.

The fact that you have an opinion doesn't mean that your opinion is correct or will be socially acceptable. This isn't always the case. In fact, some of the greatest minds in history were socially ostracised for their beliefs and opinions, even though these were eventually found to be factually correct. Challenging peoples' beliefs is frequently met with resistance. Never try to force your opinion on anyone else or demand that they do something because 'you' think it is correct. Yes, talk to people, inform them, persuade them. However, your argument needs to be able to withstand criticism, and you must be prepared to stand by your conviction.

I can think of numerous times in my life where I have been attacked for having a different opinion than someone else. And to be honest, I probably have attacked someone else for having a different opinion than me.

When we see family members or friends broadcasting a dissenting thought, we have no problem correcting them. It sometimes turns into a verbal altercation, and in some rare cases, it can even turn physical. Emotions run high, and ultimately you find yourself so angry that this person looks at something differently than you do.

Of course, there are extreme cases where dissenting thought is so in left field, it does warrant a reaction. People who advocate harm or discrimination to others are not in this conversation, and as much as they have a right to voice their beliefs, they do not have a right to wish bad on another person, and those opinions are dead wrong.

Now, people are verbally abusive towards those who feel differently than them because they cannot wrap their minds around HOW someone could feel differently than another person. People also downright ignore the dissenting opinion by either talking on the phone, or having a side conversation while the dialogue they disagree with is happening.

The same case applies with students of a particular university who protested against the Citizenship Amendment Act. It's sickening that these same students, who claim that they go to college to broaden their horizons and hear different opinions, then turn around and disrespect them. A different opinion is a different opinion, no? If presented respectfully and based on facts, then why are they throwing stones every single time they hear something they don't like, or clamouring for a safe space when someone shatters their secure bubble of facts? I thought college was for learning and growing, not for casting different souls into exile because they are just that, different.

Verbal persecution is persecution. When you want to debate about someone's opinion, stick to the issue at hand. Do not go into personal attacks, and do not start being arrogant or nasty because a person does not agree with you. Do not ignore the person like you are trying to ignore the annoying kid you graduated with at the mall. Differing opinions is what this country is built on, regardless whether you agree with them or not. Open your mind and listen to them. Respect them. Be thankful that we can have them at all.

I would like to end this chapter by stating that one should form his or her own opinions without getting influenced. And that's all that you need to do to survive at the end of each day.

Life is long and one should be chill with one's opinions.

Note - Learn to take some criticism. For God's sake.

CHAPTER SIX

SOCIETAL RANT

*"Jo maza apni pehchan se jeene me hain,
Wo kisi ki parchai banne mein nahi."*

Wikipedia defines society as, "a group of individuals involved in persistent social interaction, or a large social group sharing the same spatial or social territory, typically subject to the same political authority and dominant cultural expectations".

I'm going to spread this chapter across four sections for better understanding-

- The first section will be pertaining to the love that I have for my city
- The second one deals with the importance of living in a society
- The third section is going to be kind of a roast
- The last and final section, however, will be an emotional one.

<u>LUCKNOW</u>

Lucknow is a city which has always been regarded as the epitome of class and beauty. I have lived here all my life. Lucknow has an enormous amount of both Hindu and Muslim population. The city has been well known throughout history for it's chikan handicrafts and mouth watering cuisine across time. If you are a fan of Kebabs, Tunday will be your forever favourite. If you are a man of grace and prefer Biryani like myself, then Idrees Biryani in Nakhas will be your go-to place. If you are into Kulcha and Nahari, make sure that Mubeen's is at your speed dial. On the vegetarian front, we have Sardar Chole Bature at Anand Chauraha near Lalbagh, garlic fried rice at Motimahal, Punjabi thali at Aryan's and Nainital Momos at Gomtinagar. If you have a sweet tooth, we got you covered. You can try the evergreen Prakash Kulfi at Aminabad and the Makhan Malai stalls at Gol Darwaza in the Chowk area of Lucknow.

(Sidenote - The typist of this book is salivating already)

According to well renowned historians, it is said that Lakshmana, who was the younger brother of Lord Rama, laid the foundation of Lakshmanpur (now Lucknow). Mentioning in case the city is renamed after the elections.

Over the course of time, Lucknow was ruled by the Delhi Sultanate, Sharqi Sultanate (never heard of them), Nawabs (obviously, that's why the name 'city of nawabs') and finally by the British Raj.

Under the rule of the Nawabs, the city became North India's cultural capital. The living standard of people improved and art including music and dance flourished. Construction of numerous monuments took place, some of which include the Bara Imambara, the Chota Imambara, the Rumi Darwaza and the Teelay wali masjid (rename alert). Lucknow was the city which coined the term 'Ganga-

Jamuni Tehzeeb' referring to the religious harmony between the Hindu-Muslim culture. Ofcourse, all of it went to the dogs after the whole Babri Masjid demolition incident took place. However, the whole incident is done and dusted as the rightful section got the land. Kudos.

Lucknow was one of the major centres of the Indian Rebellion of 1857 and actively participated in India's national movement, emerging as a strategically important North Indian city.

Visit the Residency in Lucknow for a better understanding of Lucknow's involvement in 1857's rebellion.

The city's contemporary culture is the result of the amalgamation of the Hindu and Muslim rulers who ruled the city simultaneously. Modern day Lucknowites are well known for their polite and polished way of speaking, which is noticed by visitors.

Zari and Zardozi are the two indispensable z's in Lucknow's cultural heritage. The city is full of such craftsmen who are excellent at handicrafts. Unfortunately, this tradition is on the verge of dying due to the modern textile sector popping up with ready-made cloth and garments.

Lucknowites are known for their enormous love of flying kites. Growing up, it was a thing that jamghat meant flying kites from morning till evening and getting two shades darker with all the sun tan. The advent of PUBG and TikTok has taken away people's sheer love for flying kites. The whole concept of patangaazi has taken a back seat, which is also good in a way, now that people are more consumed with their work as compared to whatever.

Lucknow's unofficial language is Hindustani. It's a classical combination of the fineness of Hindi and the class of Urdu. Sweet as Chappan Bhog's mishti.

I have lived in Lucknow for my entire life. It's the city where I was born, and I've seen it evolve over the years. The urbanisation has converted the 'City of Nawabs' into a metropolitan place. However, the legacy remains intact.

Also, Lucknow is Ayushman Khurana's favourite shooting city.

No seriously.

Every second film of his is set in Lucknow.

I guess, the shooting rebates are the reason.

Living in a society has its pros and cons. Living in a society that has evolved with time makes you cultured and grounded. You learn social skills and get aware of the reality by living in a society. You see the good and the ugly, and you choose who you want to be. Furthermore, you sit down with people from all walks of life. People of different opinions and varying political ideologies sit together at the chai tapri and discuss their day. You get to see people from all walks of life. When that annual society function or some sort of meetup gets arranged, everyone for once forgets their differences and gel out with each other. It's either the love or the alcohol which plays the part.

Society should be regarded as a place which helps in the evolution of a person. Society also shapes your ideologies and your views on politics, religion and life. Society is meant to be a place which makes you open-minded and accepting of other people's reality. Society should cultivate the thoughts of peace and harmony, of love and compassion, of hard work and excellence.

This is what society should do.

Is it doing it?

Answer - Probably Not.

Society is a very elegant term. Let me resort to the Indian way of saying it - 'samaaj'.

I think that the following section will be easily palatable to the readers if I use the translated version of the word.

Here goes my rant.

Reader's discretion is advised.

Society is a place where you are judged and commented upon right from the moment you emerge out of your mother's womb. If you are a boy, pure ghee laddus are the way to go. If by chance you are a girl, laddus are out of the equation. You are commented upon for your skin colour. If you are dusky or dark or fair, people are going to comment on it. Because that's the way things go about in our society.

People comment on every thing, your colour, your religion, your caste, your sexual orientation, your height, your weight, your appearance, your academic achievements, your financial success.

Literally everything.

And they will find a way to make you feel sad and down and depressed.

Growing up, you are judged for your academic performance. At least, that was the case with me. I was an average student throughout my school life. Comparison with other kids is the worst thing a parent can do. However, in my case, my parents were understanding enough that they never compared me with other children on the academic front. I feel the reason might be that both of them belong to the profession of education and hence understand what goes in the minds of students. However, my relatives who had kids of my age always compared their marks with mine. This comparison made me feel shitty throughout my school life. If you are a slow learner and take time to process things, you are nicknamed as 'duffer' or 'dumb'. People don't understand that these small things end up being the leading cause of anxiety and depression in teenagers. If you are an average or below average student in school, you are shamed. However, if you are one of those brilliant students, you are still at a loss. People get jealous and cannot fathom your success. More than the people around you, it's your parents who end up commenting and judging you.

"*Dimag bahut hai bacche mein, bas mehnat nahi karta hai*" becomes every parents' sacred line.

If you are brought up in a middle class family like myself, then I hope you can relate.

When you arrive at the verge of adolescence, and you get pimples and acne as a result of puberty, you're judged. This time for your appearance.

If you have acne, you are given names.

If you are too skinny, you are given names.

If you are slightly overweight, you are given names.

If you are an introvert, you are given names.

If you have an extrovert and outgoing personality, you are given names.

If you fail, you are given names.

If you succeed, you are given names.

Reading in Vicky Kaushal's voice: *Sala ye dukh kahe khatam nahi hota hai be.*

You are even shamed if you don't opt for the science stream in your senior classes at school.

I mean what the f*ck.

But assuming that somehow you get through your school life, and you think that the societal norms would no longer be applicable to you, and you can chill, my friend, the game has just begun.

If you are a boy and have a metrosexual way of living in terms of your lifestyle and choices, you are called 'girlish'. If you like to keep long hair or anything that the society identifies as 'feminine', you are mocked. Derogatory remarks are hurled upon you for your opinions if you express them publicly. You are made fun of when you get KT in your semester exams. People mock you when you don't qualify that national entrance test for a particular college.

If you are a woman, I'm sorry to tell you that no matter how perfect and beautiful you are, we will find a way to make things difficult for you. I apologise that this needs stating, but a woman gets judged by the society from her childhood days. The oppression that a man faces is nothing in comparison to what a woman has to go through every day. Forget about outsiders, your parents and family members comment on the way you sit, your hair, your posture, your physical features etc. If you are happy and cheerful, you are termed as 'bubbly'. If you get mood swings when you are on your periods, you are asked to calm down as if nothing is wrong. A man can flash his junk in public and pee on the road and no one seems to have any issue with that, but a girl wearing a deep neck becomes the talk of the town. If you have opinions and say things, you are touted as the 'diva'. Wearing what you want isn't something that we can allow as a society. You are shamed for wearing short skirts and applauded when you wear Indian. You are expected to be graceful 24*7. Furthermore, you are given education not to empower you, but to get you better 'rishtas'. Less money is spent on your education and more on your dowry. You are forced to wear a hijab. You are asked to stay away from boys. You are shamed if you get a boyfriend. You are expected to remain silent if someone misbehaves with you. You are constantly made to feel small. You are denied to touch anything of religious significance during your menstrual cycle. You are expected to be beautiful but not bold.

If you are a guy, and you lose your virginity before marriage, you are regarded as a stud in your circle. However, if we see a girl holding a guy's hand, she is slut-shamed.

Mother-in-law's have their favourite dialogue ready for their daughters-in-law at every moment. The moment her boy argues with her over something, she immediately taunts the wife by saying *"Is ladki ne mere bete ko fasa rakha hai "*.

What?

What if the boy was responsible for his actions?

No, no.

How can the man be wrong?

The woman is to be blamed. She is the culprit.

It's a sad thing to see a couple getting separated and going through a divorce. But I thought about it and realised that it is the woman who is termed as the 'home wrecker' and becomes the divorcee, while the man gets married asap to the girl next door.

We always hold women responsible for anything bad that takes place because that's what we are.

A sexist, patriarchal society which will by every means try to slam you down.

When you get a respectable job and start making your livelihood, and you think you can finally live in peace as the society will stop judging you, you receive the biggest surprise of your life. Society with its horrendous norms still treats you the same way but in a more passive-aggressive manner. Because now it is all about the status game. The number of figures in your salary will decide your status in the society. If you earn less, you are termed a 'loser'. If you earn a handsome amount, you are seen as an arrogant person. If you stay in a small house and ride a bike you are considered a miser whereas if you built a nice house and buy a big car, it is believed that you are showing off. No one wants to acknowledge the sleepless nights and the sheer amount of dedication and efforts you put through to get successful. Everyone considers that you got lucky. You get married and settle down in life. But those close to you want to see some drama and try to ignite some sort of conflict between you and your spouse. If somehow you withstand all of that and feel that it's all over then my friend you are living in a bubble. You'll get kids in the future, and they will be the target of societal oppressive ways, and the loop continues.

Society shames your religion too. If you are a Hindu living in a Muslim dominated area or vice versa you are made to feel an outsider as if you don't belong there. You are not represented with respect. Your views are neglected, and you are made to feel small among the majority. You are constantly reminded that the place doesn't belong to you. The judgement can be direct or indirect. People don't call you at their place on festivals. You are made to feel alone and are tormented till you leave that particular area or surrounding.

"We are a secular country", this statement is only valid in the pages of the Indian Constitution, not in reality.

This rant reminds me of a beautiful but hard hitting poem by **Erin Hanson** -

Welcome to society,
We hope you enjoy your stay,
And please feel free to be yourself,
As long as it's in the right way,
Make sure you love your body,
Not too much or we'll tear you down,
We'll bully you for smiling,
And then wonder why you frown,
We'll tell you that you are worthless,
That you shouldn't make a sound,
And then cry with all the others,
As you're buried in the ground,
You can fall in love with anyone,
As long it's who we choose,
And we'll let you have your opinions,
But please shape them to our views,
Welcome to society,
We promise that we won't deceive,
And one more rule now that you're here,
There's no way you can leave.

This society has made up some problematic laws for every section of individuals. This society will judge a couple for holding hands in the public and make derogatory remarks on them, while the same society will shut its eyes if a woman gets raped on the road. Society enjoys seeing people fail so that they can feel better about themselves. This society becomes the cause for conflicts in relationships. This society is keen on finding flaws in people.

I may look like a person who is arrogant because of my sheer hatred towards society.

Laying some more light on that-

We often look at arrogance as a bad thing. If a person takes pride in what they are great at, people feel that the person is arrogant. The second you start looking at arrogance as a bad thing, what's actually happening is that you are being envious of someone and start judging them, and that's not necessarily good. If you think someone is arrogant, it's simply the case of being judgemental. No one means to be arrogant, it's just that they are inherently insecure that they just double down on what they think are their qualities. I am an insecure person.

I am insecure about my money, my studies, and my future job prospects.

And it's okay to accept that.

This society wants you to be insecure and people are, that's the truth. But the quicker you accept the fact that you are insecure, the better it is for you.

I think that people don't accept their flaws and everyone on the inside feels that he or she is an idiot, and they do anything to reflect the opposite and that just ends up being the arrogance that people witness. People are not arrogant because they want to make a statement or boast about their accomplishments. People are arrogant because they want to protect their own self-esteem. And there's nothing wrong with it.

But

But

But,

Making it a daily ritual is not sustainable because in the ultimate battle, karma wins.

Use your insecurities as your shield, not your sword.

Be arrogant not to impress, but to protect.

Society pushes you to achieve your goals quickly and grow up faster. You are expected to complete your studies and get the best job out there and start earning, which isn't necessarily all bad, but the repercussions of this peer pressure can be fatal.

Patience and the realisation that life is long, and you don't have to be in a hurry is the key of life. Just keep working and doing your best, and you'll realise that things will eventually work out. They always do. For some people slightly early, for some people a little later, but eventually everything works out. Patience as a virtue is something that I've learnt immensely now. This realisation has led me to accept my flaws and work on them. People are flawed, and it's okay to acknowledge that. The sooner you embrace your imperfections, the better it would eventually be for you.

Let society not tell you that you are flawed or imperfect, you can realise it yourself.

And life is too long to get bogged down by negativity,

Remember once a drunk man holding a hair comb as a mic said, *"Humari filmon ki tarah humari life mein bhi end mein sab theek ho jata hai, aur agar sb theek na ho to vo the end nahi hai doston, picture abhi baaki hai mere dost"*.

Article 15 of the Indian Constitution states that the state shall not discriminate against any citizen on the grounds of race, religion, caste, sex or place of birth.

This society looks down upon you on the basis of your caste. We would think that it's the 21st century and the world has evolved and issues like caste discrimination aren't prevalent in our society any more but let me tell you that we have not gone one step further in this path over the last hundred of years. We are still narrow-minded. Furthermore, we'll not sit and eat next to a person who is of a different caste. It's sad, but the reality is that many people are not allowed to enter religious places just because other people consider them to belong to an inferior caste. And it's not the case with a particular religion, actually I think it's not about religion at all. People from all walks of life, from all religions, from all socio-economic backgrounds have inherited this from their forefathers, the very seed of discrimination. I think that we should all admit to the fact that our forefathers and ancestors were not completely right in any way, shape or form. They were oppressive, sexist and unaware. I'm not saying that they were deliberately wrong because that was the time during which society taught them to be oppressive in their ways and mannerisms. However, times are changing now and one should continue evolving as opposed to sticking with the thousand-year-old traditions that some of our ancestors came up with.

Some people cite their religious textbooks regarding the existence of the caste system and why it's important. The Early Vedic period divided people in four sections viz Brahmanas, Kshatriyas, Vaishyas and Shudras. But that division was made up because of the job that they do and their social responsibility. It was not about having a certain surname. People now take a certain pride in their surnames.

"We are Tripathi",

"We are Rastogi",

"We are Pathan",

"We are Gupta",

I mean, what the hell.

This act of boasting about your surname just makes you seem like an arrogant prick.

Two individuals who love each other cannot get married because the pandit or the maulvi said that their caste is not the same. We live in a society where you can marry a tree but cannot marry a person of a different caste or background.

The only solution to this problem can be the fact that education and values should be given to the upcoming generation. We as a nation question why we are still regarded as a Third World country, the reason lies in the fact that we have a very narrow mindset as a nation and a society. Close mindedness and the unwillingness to adapt and learn is the dealbreaker for our nation. Our brain is like a rock, not a sponge. We avoid the absorption of new ideas and want to stick to the customs and traditions of the ancient era.

This narrow-minded and cruel society cannot get over the fact that homosexuality is a natural thing, and it exists.

Baba Ramdev made a very potent statement in 2018 which condenses in the following manner, "Homosexuality can be cured by yoga".

WTF?

Is it a disease that needs a cure?

People like him that are so influential and still make such stupid and nonsensical statements should be banned, not comedians like Vir Das who have the balls to say the right thing.

I'm not a hypocrite, and hence I'll call out the bullshit on the other part too.

A Maulana in Kerala cited the Sharia law, which states that "any sort of intimate or physical relationship between the people of the same gender is haram".

People cannot fathom the fact that no heterosexual person can be converted into a homosexual and vice versa. It is as natural to be homosexual as it is to be heterosexual.

Homosexuality is not a disease, not a sin and definitely not against the nature. PERIOD.

We as a society and as a nation are still homophobic and will continue to be so if we don't normalize its existence.

Anything that has not been prevalent or talked about in our society for a long time, when it emerges out, we often regard it as the ill effects of the western world. Our society still considers it a taboo subject and is ashamed of talking about it. I think one of the main reasons for homophobia is the lack of sex education in our country. We are the second most populous country in the world with an overgrowing population, and view talking about sex and educating people about it as shameful.

We shame the gay, we shame the lesbian, we shame the transgender, we shame the bisexual.

Many times, I have seen people using obscene and derogatory terms such as 'hijra', 'chakka', 'meetha' etc. for people of the transgender community. We think very less of them and think that they are ill-mannered, and sometimes that is true. It is true that if a certain section of the society is oppressed for centuries, it is bound to become agitated and angry.

Lord Shiva is known as ***Ardhanarishvara*** for a reason. If God himself acknowledges the fact that the lines between gender can be blurred, then why not us?

Being a heterosexual man, I don't understand how it feels to love a person of the same gender, but I do understand the fact that love is love. I, too, used to be a homophobic person. All throughout my childhood and teenage years, I considered it a bad thing and used to casually comment on the transgender community. But with time and learning about the aspects of their lives, I've become empathetic towards all communities. I'm an avid supporter of LGBTQ rights, as one should be. Many of us want to support them but don't do it publicly because of many reasons.

I understand that.

If you cannot support them, then at least don't shame them.

Empathise with people.

That's how we will build a better society.

The amount of pressure that our traditional Indian society puts upon us is uncalled-for. Sometimes this pressure brings out the best in us and is surprisingly beneficial. However, most of the time, this peer pressure breaks us down and bogs us in the dark pit of self-doubt and anxiety. We start feeling neglected, we feel that we don't fit in and hence resort to doing stupid stuff to be a part of the conversation. The constant comparison with a more successful person leads to nowhere, but a dark place in terms of the mental health of an individual. People are unapologetic and least accepting of other people, they make judgements over your issues and lower your self-confidence. A person who is constantly neglected by society and constantly abused ends up in the dichotomy of life where on one end his mental peace is gone and on the other end he loses the sense of his own perspective.

We have found the tendency to conformity in our society so strong that reasonably intelligent and well-meaning young people are willing to call white as black. Young individuals in our society are forced to act and feel a certain way. Society enjoys dictating how our youth should behave. The pressure placed on teens to meet a certain requirement leads to harmful outcomes. Although some pressures are only experienced by a particular gender and not the other, some are endured by both, and it is only fair to say that both of them feel the pressure of fitting in with societal norms.

Although I feel that society as a whole is becoming more accepting to people who may not fit the stereotype, there is still pressure to conform. There is still, and always be, the pressure to look the same as your peers; wear what they wear, do as they do, speak as they speak. There is always a pressure to emulate what society sees as the standard for your gender or orientation. There will always be people who will ridicule those who have a different mindset or those who have contrary opinions. The fear of ridicule is what makes most people desire to fit in, sometimes to the point of breaking. People, not just girls, not just boys, not just gays, not just transgender, not just lesbians will do anything to fit in and go to extreme lengths to do it. And that's all where the problem arises.

Why should one try to fit in?

If you are a good human being who has different views, be happy because you are different. That's what makes you special. Don't try to fit in, and you'll soon realise that society is not that much of a bad place after all. There have always been those rare people who don't try to fit in. They are those who are okay with who they are and what society has to say about them, who do not care what they should be, but care about who they are. And I believe that to be the best form of existence.

It's fair to say that in today's day and age, people experience many pressures from society to look and behave a certain way. Some pressures hit a particular community, either way our culture strives to create clones of what they believe people should resemble.

Society has become so fake that the truth bothers people. You relax on a plane, even though you don't know the pilot. You relax on a ship, even though you don't know the captain. You relax on a bus, even though you don't know the driver. Why don't you relax in life, knowing that the universe is in control?

This is such a brief life - doing what you truly care for is the only way to make your life worthwhile. If you know how to handle your thoughts and emotions, there will be no such things such as stress, anxiety or tension that leads to depression for you.

When a life is born, that in itself an achievement. Life is a combination of sad and happy emotions. A life is born in a society. A society is meant to have some fixed rules that need to be followed. As we grow up, we are shaped to follow those rules. We are taught to achieve a status in society. So, from our childhood, we start planning things the way we are told. There comes the word 'depression'.

Depression.

What is DEPRESSION?

No, I don't mean it in terms of the geographical concept or Brent Rambo's music video.

I'm talking about clinical depression, the one which messes up with your head.

BTW, have you noticed that every time you google search the word 'depression', the first image that the algorithm shows up is a black and white image of a girl holding her forehead. Not worth mentioning, but I felt the compulsion to mention it.

So, what is depression? There are many theses and studies that vary in terms of defining depression as a concept?

Depression is - fundamentally you expected something to happen, but it didn't happen the way you thought, and you are simply against what is happening, that's all, or maybe you are against a person, or maybe you are against the whole situation, maybe you are against life itself. Accordingly, the depression will run deeper and deeper.

But why are you against something? Only because things didn't go the way you want them to be, isn't it?

Why should the whole world go your way? Please know that the world does not go your stupid way. It is never going to be your way. With failure there is always success, so with success there can be failures too. So when we enjoy success, happiness with an open heart, then why is failure and sorrow not accepted with the same heart?

So either you have no faith in the creator or you have no acceptance or both, and you have a hyper-sensitive ego. That's why we get depressed. So much pain is caused by one to another. Why do the rules which are made to make us live happily take a life?

Now comes the point to think - what are we heading to?

Should we force our kids to be stronger individuals, or do we fight for a change in our societal values?

The first step is shifting our values. Putting things like creativity and individuality above fitting in is essential in making a change. Society needs to stop giving orders to our generation on how to look and act and instead of prescribing us with a path to follow, let us make our own. People, especially young people, should be free of pressure to look a certain way, act a certain way, behave a certain way, and think a certain way. We should not be robots, programmed to carry out what a big boss wants. We all need to learn to want better for ourselves, but at the same time be okay with ourselves. Likewise, we need to learn not to go against our own feelings for what society wants us to feel.

Grooming should be done in a way that we develop a personality that is ready to face the world. Life is not always going to remain the same. Nothing is permanent (not even relations). Relations change, we lose our loved ones, as this is the truth of life. Things will come and go, so be stable and handle them, be prepared for them. Be strong to live the way the things come up with you.

Why not groom in such a way that we believe in 'karma' ?

When people insult you, don't be offended, don't take it personally, but do listen to their words. They are telling you how they see the world, and they are telling you the exact negative qualities that they possess. The 'law of mirror' states that one can only see what's in them, regardless, if it is what is actually present in reality or not. So high time for us to think about how to groom our future generations and our children. Make them strong for both ups and downs of society. Show them the truth of life. Make them feel that no matter what happens in their future for us, they will always be precious.

Everybody's requirements from life are different.

So what is required is to talk to people, spread love and make a new rule which makes everybody feel that nothing is more important in this world than life.

You should keep on moving with life and believe in yourself to act well. Be supportive and bring happiness around.

Society is because of us, we are not for society.

Guru Dutt rightly said, *"Ye duniya agar mil bhi jaye to kya hai"*.

CHAPTER SEVEN

COUNTRY: EXPECTATIONS VS REALITY

"Religion wala jo column hota hai, us mein hum bold aur capital mein INDIAN likhte hain."

Before starting this chapter, I would like to present some love letters that I wrote-

To,

The Government of any state in India,

You know that being afraid of you is not the same thing as supporting you. Right?

You know that dominance and government are not the same thing. Right?

And don't pretend like you don't know that we are afraid of you.

There are literally hostages who have Stockholm syndrome, who have the same expression as our actors do when they click selfies with leaders from our government.

Your biggest achievement is that you made it basically impossible for us to argue with you.

And you confuse that with us agreeing with you, and that's not the same thing.

Thank you,

A citizen of India.

To Young Politicians,

You know who you are.

The ones who say party line stuff in public and then try to be progressive in private.

You know you're cool on Twitter, and then you say hateful stuff in speeches.

You know that we can see through you. Right?

We see you switch around and run between the political party and who you really want to be.

Kho Kho is still one of our national sports.

We recognize that pattern.

To the Congress,

When are you going to realise that it's basically all over for you.

I'm sorry. Just accept it, it's all over.

You're dinosaurs who are stuck in arctic icebergs.

You're beautifully preserved but technically dead.

When are you going to stop trying to shove your 50-year-old prodigal son down our throats?

Go away.

If for nothing else just to mess with people of the government.

And why do you want to come back?

Look at Bill Gates.

He retired with grace, and you have made way more money than that guy.

Forget Apple, you're literally the most profitable company in the world.

That's what you should do.

Just get Chinese people to make you phones. And if you are looking for Chinese people, you can now find them within our territory.

To The Aam Aadmi Party,

Here's a question for you.

Hey, where are you guys?

You're still a thing?

Still going on?

Because you kinda went from being like, "Okay, we are going to listen to everyone and fix everything" to just being like, "We're going to listen to that one guy and fix that one thing".

You're like Osho without all the sex or the fun.

I am not saying that you're a cult. But you listen to one guy and wear matching hats.

To millennials,

I love that you're getting involved in politics, can you please also read up a little.

No generation is equipped to deal with more information than you guys.

So it sucks to see you guys at protests just to be like, "Ya man we're here to protest against CABC...BACC...BBC".

Read some info, would you?

Everybody in the nation is terrified of you.

Politicians are terrified because you can see through them.

News channels are terrified because you don't watch them.

Intellectuals are terrified because you know more stuff than them.

To intellectuals/opinion makers/people with large twitter followings/writers/mout pieces/the lecture circuits,

I realise that what you are saying is important but do you have to be so dislikable?

Oh My God, you know no one likes you.

Reading or listening to your opinion is like eating broccoli dipped in kale sauce.

I know it's good for me, but it just leaves such a rotten taste.

And you've got this notion that, because of your achievements people should respect you.

Let me break it down for you.

In today's India nobody respects you.

I don't like you and I'm one of you.

Well that was a lot.

India is an awesome nation. We as Indians take great pride in the fact that we are the oldest civilisation in the world. We have snow-clad mountains, we got beautiful beaches, great food and a hell lot of people. Right from J&K to Kankayumari's tip, India is a land of culture and traditions. We as Indians have inherited a massive amount of cultural heritage. India is the land of all religions, all colours, all castes, all sexes and all mentalities. All of that is great, and we should be proud of that. But what we should not be proud of is the various issues that are stopping our country from becoming the best version of itself. Let's not forget the flaws that are making us really lack in the areas of humanity. We suffer from mentality issues, prejudices, stereotypes and hypocrisy. Only when we rise above it all can we shape our country better. I'm going to address some of these issues in this chapter, hopefully I will try my best to be real and positive.

CORRUPTION

"Power tends to corrupt, and absolute power corrupts absolutely."

Corruption may be defined as "Misuse of authority as a result of consideration of personal gain, which need not be monetary".

Corruption in Indian society has prevailed from time immemorial in one form or the other. History reveals that it was present even during the Mauryan empire. Great scholar Kautilya had also indicated forty different kinds of corruption in his contemporary society. Hence, corruption is not a new phenomenon in our country. Corruption promotes illegality, inequality, injustice, inconsistency and inefficiency in public conduct and behaviour. The basic inception of corruption started with our opportunistic leaders, who have already done greater damage to our nation. People who work on the right principles are unrecognized and considered to be foolish in the modern world. Corruption in India is a result of the connection between bureaucrats, politicians and criminals. Earlier bribes were taken for getting the wrong things done, but now bribes are paid for getting the right things done at the right time. Further, corruption has become something respectable in India, because respectable people are involved in it.

Corruption destroys the moral fabric of the society and erodes the faith of the common man in the legitimacy of the political and administrative setup. I would say that corruption is the cancer that is hurting our nation and its economy very badly. Demonetization was the first step towards making India corruption free. And we all know how that turned out.

Corruption, in one form or another, is a worldwide global phenomenon. But everyone admits that corruption is something ugly, immoral and detestable. Unfortunately, in our country, corruption has become a part of life. It has entered the very roots of Indian society. Our ministers are corrupt; our officers are corrupt; and so are we.

Corruption is spread over society in several forms. The major ones are:

- Bribe - money offered in cash or kind or gift or under the pretext of *kharcha pani* as inducement to procure illegal or dishonest action in favour of the giver.
- Nepotism - undue favour from holds of patronage to relatives.
- Misappropriation - using others money for one's own case.
- Patronage - wrong support/encouragement given by patrons and thus misusing the position.

People are not corrupt, they're just innocent of integrity. Really, they don't know what it means to have a certain sense of integrity. It's simply that the very idea does not exist. It is not just in the political circle, it's across the board. Integrity does not mean just a certain set of morals and ethics. Integrity is- there are certain things, no matter what, you don't do. It's not because of your morals or ethics, but simply because of your humanity, because you have a larger sense of being human, not just you being human. So, this has to come experientially to every human being, not just the leaders, everybody. There is a serious amount of work to be done in the country.

Corruption needs immediate action as it has retarded or development. It has created the black and red money, which is not available for productive investment. In spite of the liberalisation of the economy, corruption comes in the way of foreign direct investment inflows. In short, it has become a threat to the national security of India. The serious consequences of corruption have created the need to fight it from all angles at the earliest.

The primary solutions that I can come up with in my head are as follows-

- The first solution is that the citizens should fight corruption more strongly. In the past, the perception was that a citizen will have to bribe a public servant if he wants to get a benefit, which was illegal. But today, we have reached a stage where even if the legitimate requirements are satisfied, the citizens have to bribe the public servant to get the benefit quickly and without any hassle. These attitudes need to change. The public itself has to stand strong against corruption. If we stop bribing, then most certainly will the level of corruption step down in our nation.

- A family attachment is an important cause of corruption. A family person feels that he should earn enough not only for himself and his lifetime but also for his children, grandchildren and perhaps the next seven generations. So he requires enormous accumulation of wealth. We all know that there is no legitimate way of earning exponentially large sums of money, and thus the person falls in the pit of bribery and becomes a bait to corruption. In this situation, a strong youth movement in the country can help reduce corruption at a family level.

- We have evolved in our country's red tape ridden elaborate system leading to enormous delays. This probably makes the common man consider paying bribes as 'speed money'. So the system of governance should be changed. Transparency should be a keyword in the public offices. Technological development can be the best solution in this respect. Online transactions would reduce the need for the citizens to visit public offices and government departments.

- The law enforcement authorities also have a crucial role to play in this context. The only thing, which has to be ensured, is proper, impartial, and unbiased use of various Anti-corruption Acts to take strong, deterrent prompt and timely legal action against the offenders, irrespective of their political connections, and money or muscle power.

- Simplified forms and procedures reduce dependency of the users on intermediaries. This will also minimise the government-citizen interfaces and reduce the potential for corruption.

- A value based leadership encourages effective governance. Positive values like compassion, helping others and truthfulness etc. help to build and develop a society. These values will not only curb people's attraction towards corrupt practises, but also improve their rotten mindsets.
- The implementation of policies like anti-poverty programmes should be corruption-free. Only a small fraction of the benefit in these programmes accrues to the target population. There should be control checkpoints to find out the scope of corruption. Strict measures should be taken against those enforcing programmes only with the intention of making money out of it.
- Good practises of organisations in the corporate sector should be highlighted. Regulatory mechanisms should be strengthened.
- Another effective way of curtailing corruption could be to introduce a method which will enable political parties to secure electoral funds in a bona fide manner, or the central government may finance elections through an election fund.
- The media has to perform quite an active role in exposing the causes of corruption. It should not be just doing the sting operations but also expose bad practises to the public, making them aware and compelling them to avoid such incidents in the future. The strategy of building public opinion against corruption can be effectively implemented through mass media.

I have grinded my mind and could come up with these solutions which I think will prove beneficial in the course of bringing corruption to a step-down in our nation. India can progress only if there is good governance, there can be no good governance unless moral values are inculcated in the people. There is no way out but to change the system if it is not value-based.

CORRUPTION IS REAL.

CORRUPTION IS FATAL.

SAY NO TO CORRUPTION.

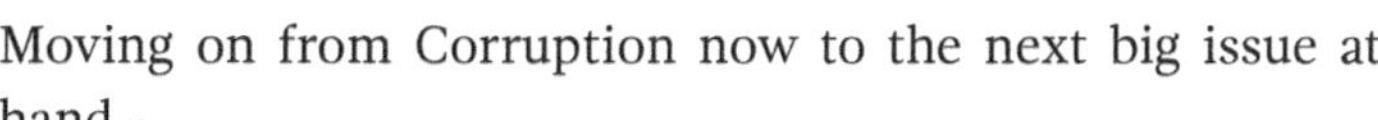

Moving on from Corruption now to the next big issue at hand -

VIOLENCE TOWARDS WOMEN

NO MEANS NO, how difficult is it to understand?

India is a country where goddesses rule the star-spangled pantheon of deities, riding tigers, slaying evil and showering good fortune. Bollywood heroines rule Indian hearts. Indira Gandhi, TIME Magazine's ninth most powerful woman in the last century, was also India's second-longest serving Prime Minister and the rare female head of state in her time. Despite these pedestals for females in India, what's behind rape and sexual violence in India, and why does this paradox exist?

It was a crime that shook the country, the gang rape and murder of Jyoti Singh. The twenty three year old was attacked by five men on a bus in New Delhi in 2012. The case triggered mass protests across the nation. The conversation on rape became stronger. It was back in 2012, and it's been almost a decade and India still remains one of the most dangerous countries for women.

According to the data analysis done by the Central Bureau of Investigation(CBI) in 2019, a woman is raped every fifteen minutes in India. A report from The Ministry of Home Affairs shows that thirty-four thousand women were raped in 2018. And only twenty-seven percent of the reported cases led to convictions. Researchers say that the actual number of assaults are likely far higher, as people are reluctant to report sexual attacks. The violence girls and women face often begins even before they are born and continues over the course of their lives in homes, institutions and public spaces. Violence in the womb gets normalised because of the social and cultural factors that continually emphasise male privilege in patriarchy.

According to the NRCB, the number of cases filed against sexual violence have dropped from 95.4 percent in 2013 to 86.6 percent of all investigated and guilty cases in 2021. The laws in our country regarding sexual violence against women are so alarming.

For instance, rape within marriage is not considered a crime. And only recently did acid attacks on women become a crime.

I mean, seriously?

In curbing and understanding the problems of sexual violence in India, it is important to recognise that there is not one isolated factor. There are a confluence of issues and reasons, each reinforcing the other. Ranging from a lack f sexual education to societal norms that entrench gender inequality to inadequate legal deterrence, the issues run deep. Addressing the issue requires a multifaceted approach.

For often than not, we question the victim and not the offender.

Why are women in our country so regularly blamed for being raped or sexually assaulted?

Though victim-blaming defies reason, the belief that women provoke or deserve sexual assault is widespread. Explanations range from "boys will be boys" to "jeans cause rape", but men themselves are rarely blamed.

A recent documentary by The Quint explored social attitudes that normalise rape, presenting it as "consensual". What appears to be an oxymoron, points to a macabre explanation: beyond legality, sexual assault takes place on deeper, varied, meanings based on social and cultural context. Often, justifying rape is merely the tip of a larger "iceberg" of patriarchal attitudes.

In our society, skirts and pants are considered "inappropriate clothing" for women, while wearing saree or salwar-kameez is considered appropriate. People think that the modern clothing for women is revealing in nature. I cannot fathom the fact that people around us believe that. It's the 21st century, for god's sake, and we are still stuck in the 1940s. Rape and other forms of sexual violence are not driven by the fact that the woman is wearing a revealing dress, it's the psyche that prevails.

How can we boast of being a great nation when a four-month-old child gets raped. It's atrocious.

Preference for modest attire might reflect preoccupations with izzat(honour) and fear of honour-related violence. Such attitudes may also indicate support for the idea that women dressed 'inappropriately' somehow deserve the shame or assault.

The so-called society blames the abused, not the abuser.

City dwellers' openness does not translate into gender-equitable attitudes. Most of them think that "women should tolerate eve teasing as a normal part of life". These morons are, in fact, slightly more likely, than rural Indians, to normalise sexual harassment. Despite perceptions that wealthier/more educated Indians are more egalitarian, sexual harassment is accepted or tolerated by about half of the Indians across gender, income and most education groups.

India's attitudes towards women reflect apathy and an acceptance of sexual harassment. The tendency to judge and police what women wear is inseparable from the normalisation of sexual harassment: both reflect a broader pattern of social control over women's bodies. People make statements like "A husband has the right to discipline his wife", thus making domestic violence prevalent. The man feels that he is entitled enough to lay his hands on his spouse. Things such as these need to change drastically. Sorry to say, but more often than not, women appear to reinforce patriarchal norms. Perhaps, some women are reluctant to voice their views, while others might endorse the status quo. Either way, prospects for gender equality seem grim.

So, is there a cure to solve the issue of violence towards women? There surely is.

- To even begin an attempt to alter this, we need a robust conversation around men, which has to begin in schools, public fora and highest offices. Boys have to be taught that it's wrong to talk disparagingly about women, feel up girls surreptitiously, make lewd remarks and leer at them. This cannot be left to parents alone. Schools are known as "temples of education" for a reason.
- It should be a part of the school curriculum for primary school onwards, where attitudes are shaped. For older students, gender sensitisation classes and tests should be made mandatory. Violence against women is so deeply rooted in our society, that this sensitisation should be prioritised as much as basic reading and writing skills. Girls must be encouraged to be strong, vocal and intolerant of transgressions, however small.

- Workplaces must crackdown on men who make sexualised jokes, even of the 'water cooler kind'. We should stop taking sexually offensive banter lightly, because it leads to desensitisation, which starts casually and eventually normalises sexual violence.

- Most importantly, public office bearers and role models need to stop blaming women for their choice of dress or work hours, because that does nothing to make India a safer place for women. Instead, it emboldens male vulturine behaviour and robs women of their potential by forcing them to cut short their work or leisure activities.

- In the meantime, the most immediate solution is to set up a special law enforcement arm that deals with sexual offences. India's police force, heavily overworked, mostly desensitised and routinely pulled in different directions, can no longer be counted on to devote the time and dedication needed to deal with this deep and wide social issue.

- The government must set up a special unit that recruits and trains officers specifically to deal with sexual offences, and create early access to doctors, forensic experts, rape survivors and psychologists. All registered offences must be dealt with by this unit within a month using fast-track courts. This will help victims feel confident in coming forward to seek justice. Predators must know that justice is swift and favourable to victims.

- India's approach to curbing sexual aggression must steer clear of diminishing women, and root out reckless patriarchal attitudes instead.

It's a good sign that our central and state governments are making strict laws with regard to violence towards women. However, it will be of no utility until we start educating our boys about how to treat women and respect them.

We are a land of Maa Durga, after all.

I think this chapter is going to be the lengthiest of all.

Next issue-

CANCEL/BAN/BOYCOTT CULTURE

If you don't know what cancel culture is, it's fine. You'll find out. You guys usually get cancelled first. Cancel culture is kind of like tribalism's weekly human sacrifice. It keeps the online volcano happy. It's a system that is so imperfect, it's almost perfect. It's imperfect people saying imperfect things that are discovered by imperfect people, who then hand out imperfect punishments. It's kind of like this big online trial where the entire jury is made up of criminals and the very defendant identifies as a judge. That is how I describe cancel culture in exactly a hundred words.

Now that we are done with that, let's try to understand the ban and boycott culture.

Let me lay out an example here: Why do we blindly follow those who address themselves as Baba, Sadhvi, Maulana or Pir? Is it because of culture or tradition or superstition? For these people, COVID is not a big issue. If it is, it can be solved by cow urine. On the other hand, when a well-read scientist (in white lab coat) advises something, we become sceptical. After more than seventy years of independence, why are we still slaves of superstitions? The superstition which says that if the thing is ancient, it is right and whatever is new or challenging, we seem to be against it. When we don't understand something or can't wrap our head around something, we immediately want to BAN it.

We don't realise that life is a maze and problems will keep arising day after day, and obviously modern problems require modern solutions (you see what I did there). We just seem to have one solution to all issues - BAN/BOYCOTT.

- Cross border tension solution - Ban Pakistani artists (Atif is the G.O.A.T)
- COVID was harsh - Ban PUBG
- Didn't like the Tanishq Ad - Ban the advertisement
- Problem of Alcohol addiction in a state - Alcohol banned
- Women's safety issues - Ban them from going out (sad but true)
- Twitter says manipulated post was shared - Ban twitter
- What is crypto, can't understand - Ban crypto

Banning is equal to controlling. Hitler rightly said, "To control people, take away their freedom little by little. Slowly but surely. Do it in secrecy before they can understand what's happening." Now, the argument rises that everybody has the freedom of speech and freedom of expression in democracy. But this freedom is not absolute. There are reasonable restrictions on freedom. The reasonable restrictions- Don't offend anyone. But, that's the issue. Because anybody can get offended over anything. You can get offended by the font of this book and I may get offended by you getting offended, and so on and so forth. Hence, there are no criteria in offence. We are so many times offended, as if taking offence is our national hobby. Be it religion, caste, region, sentiments or attachments. And what's our way of dealing with offence- ban or boycott.

Movies are easy targets for the ban and boycott culture-

- The film BOMBAY invited howls of protests from both sides of the parliament during the time of its release. It was taken off the screens in Hyderabad and Northern Karnataka.
- The 2002 Indian drama PARZANIA was banned in Gujarat. Reason? It was said that it had a pro-minority angle.
- Rajput communities held protests against movies like Jodhaa Akbar, Padmavati and Ramleela citing the historical inaccuracies that were apparently present in the film.
- The barber community got offended by the Shah Rukh Khan and Irrfan starrer BILLU BARBER.
- The Hollywood classic DA VINCI CODE was also stalled when the Christian organisations protested.
- Deepika Padukone's CHAPAK was boycotted after she joined the JNU students at a protest.

Many films were banned because they showed mirrors to the government. For example- 'Kissa Kursi Ka' was one of the first satirical films on the emergency period. The government banned it because they feared that their image would be tarnished. Gulzar's Aandhi, loosely based on Indira Gandhi's life, was also boycotted. SRK's My Name is Khan, Aamir Khan's PK, Akshay Kumar's OMG, Alia Bhatt's Sadak 2 are some of the movies that were boycotted in the recent years.

The Censor Board often makes the news for trimming down scenes in movies. However, bigger bans make news all over the world. Like, in 2018, Uttarakhand High Court asked the Centre to impose a ban on porn sites. The reason given was that these websites led to the increasing amount of rapes in the country. Even after banning them, according to the latest reports, India's porn consumption has only increased. And the thing about women's safety? The less said the better.

*God forbid you use any of my book's pages as a tissue.

<u>One more controversial point-</u> **The legalistion of Weed-**

Cannabis has been consumed since ancient times in our nation. Weed is something that can be used for recreational purposes as well as for medicinal purposes. However, weed was pushed into the drugs category by the then Prime Minister Rajiv Gandhi under American pressure. Despite that, weed is still consumed under the table and in gatherings during Holi under the pretext of thandai. This is not the way of reducing drug usage. Outright banning is neither the solution nor the soluchan (any kamlesh fans here). News anchors want to ban drugs on live TV now. Have you guys seen that? 'The Nation wants to know' guy screaming on the TV, "Drugs do, drugs do, drugs do". I can't figure out if he was asking for drugs or a ban on drugs.

Behavioural sciences have shown that information and awareness do more good than outright banning. For example- Bihar is a dry state (sale of alcohol is banned), but an underground network is still very much at play. This generally leads to corruption. Plus, the government doesn't earn any taxes. Banning is like a challenge, we take it on quite vigorously and thus we have learned to cope despite the ban. Like, when the Supreme Court ordered bars and pubs near highways not to sell alcohol (less alcohol, less accidents), a number of states renamed the highways and turned them local. So technically, not a violation of order and the alcohol lobby continues to flourish.

Ban does not take research and study into account. No planning, nothing, as it is too much work. Ban is easy, and the public also likes immediate action. So it is obvious that a ban is a nice, simple short-term solution. Perhaps that is why India is among those countries which spend the least on research and development (Source - Business Today, October 2021 issue).

Sometimes, they want bans on day-to-day things such as Oppo and Xiaomi phones under the **#boycottchineseproducts** agenda. Unfortunately, the WhatsApp University does not state facts like that China's export into India in terms of smartphones and other electronics is merely 2%. Mobile applications like TikTok and PUBG get banned. Today, Instagram Reels are being filmed on those very Chinese phones and PUBG is back.

The youth of our nation is energetic, but that energy must be channelled in the right place. But if the youth starts to think logically, it will prove to be a problem for the government. So why not distract them by urging them to seek a ban on random things.

Ban is clearly a powerful tool. Often misused. The question is, why would we do that to ourselves?

Short Answer - **Insecurity.**

Long Answer-

- Let's take an example - In Kashmir, 4G was banned for almost a year citing national security, sovereignty and integrity. This was a decision by the government and the reason was to stop the militant propaganda so that peace may thrive across the state. Even after a year, the situation still remains the same. Misunderstandings between the Kashmiris and the government have only increased. This is called **Political Insecurity.**

- Religion is a source of inspiration for many. It is a belief system. How can an ad, feature film or dialogue hurt it so easily? This is called **Religious insecurity.**

Internal fears and doubts allow ban culture to thrive. Ban and boycott have become the new normal, sadly. It is not a solution though. Even if we obey these boycotts and bans, we are no less than sheep, who blindly follow, without questioning. The solution is researching the issue, understanding it and tackling it, building a robust framework and getting alternate solutions as opposed to banning or boycotting something. It's not as easy as banning. But, it's definitely progressive.

I do realise that pointing out these issues is the easiest task, and reforming the country is completely different.

Here are 69 (NICE) changes that we desperately need in our nation. These would be enough to put us in the category of 'First World Nations' -

1. We as a nation and society should learn to respect women and make them feel safe. The nations that have stronger women are always at the top.
2. Every girl should have the Right to Live (i.e. no female infanticide), Right to Education and Right to Marry (no honour killing)
3. Good Governance. Seriously, it's the need of the hour.
4. Free and efficient healthcare for the underprivileged. I have seen many close ones suffer from fatal diseases and eventually die due to the lack of funds.

5. Retirement age of politicians. This change should be a must. When developed nations like the US and UK can do it, then why not us. We require the youth to run the country, not some problematic seventy-year-old with a beer belly.
6. Corruption free India. There should be no need to pay a bribe for your rights.
7. Control over black money. I mean real control. Not some futile publicity stunt that was 'Demonetization'
8. Stricter measures for pollution control throughout the year (not just during Diwali).
9. Proper enforcement of laws. Stricter but capable.
10. Reformation of education system. 'Mitochondria is the powerhouse of the cell' seems like a cliché now.
11. A clean India! Proper rubbish (not Twitter trends) and drainage system.
12. Improved road network with no potholes or broken roads. Just the correct amount to enjoy the fantasy of being in a Zoya Akhtar road trip movie. Ude, Khule Aasman Mein Khaabon Ke Parinday....
13. A streamlined traffic system without that atrocious Akshay Kumar advertisement.
14. Improve drinking water quality. A final farewell to Hema Malini's Kent RO plug.
15. Agriculture should be encouraged, and modern agricultural techniques should be used. Dependence on monsoon should get out of the question. Everyone hates them.
16. Stricter laws should be made for the unnecessary use of private vehicles; usage of public transport should be made mandatory wherever possible. No need to complain about the ever-increasing petrol prices.

17. Power and water supply in every part of the country. There isn't a SRK happening from Swades anytime soon.
18. A mandatory education qualification should be fixed for politicians too. Statements on potatoes converting into gold will finally be gone.
19. Equality for all. Say NO to Reservation.
20. Controlled inflation. No punchline here, since economics and me don't go hand in hand.
21. Employment for all. No one should remain a 'vella'.
22. The police should be well-equipped and there should be more accountability not just in Rohit Shetty's movies but in the real world as well.
23. Legalisation of marijuana. This is a personal favour.
24. Care for the environment. Don't need Priyanka Chopra and Virat Kohli to remind us of that every year.
25. Say no to beggars. Begging is something that strictly needs to be discouraged and abolished. There should be no more space for lines like, 'ae de na', 'allah ke naam pe dede'.
26. A change in the mindset of people is highly required. The way they look at society, social norms and individuals needs a changed and sensible approach.
27. Proper disaster management.
28. Hassle-free government procedures. Indian citizens have seen many martial art movies from Korea now, you guys don't need to replicate it in the Lok Sabha any more.
29. Poverty eradication. Also, no poverty porn please: Indian Idol.
30. Increase production and usage of products that are 'Made in India. Fun Fact- Bata is not an Indian brand.
31. Solar plants and rainwater harvesting systems should be established at maximum infrastructures.

32. Unnecessary expenditure on travel and other things by the politicians should be controlled. Not naming names here.

33. A language check over politicians. OH! PLEASE. PLEASE. PLEASE.

34. Lavish expenditures on organising events on different occasions should be controlled. Not getting religious here.

35. Biasness on the basis of religion, caste, creed or gender should be eradicated. Article 25 of the Indian Constitution should be given more importance. Only then will the actual 'acche din' arrive.

36. No wastage of food anywhere. This is something that all of us should agree upon despite our differences.

37. Special economic zones should be constructed in not only metro cities but also every small city, so that people do not have to migrate to the metropolitan cities for employment.

38. More playgrounds for children. We have been using the same 1000 sq ft area for cricket and badminton growing up.

39. Adulteration should be controlled, and organic food must be easily made available.

40. Equal education and employment opportunities should be provided to people for the transgender community. I'm very happy to see the changes our government is trying to make, and hopefully it's all uphill from here. Representation of transgender in the entertainment field is getting better, thanks to the emergence of OTT platforms.

41. Job security for all.

42. Media should be more responsible. Facts should be stated without biases.

43. Punishing fake god men who beguile people in the name of God. Hate speeches should be banned.
44. Accepting the filth in the societal norms and working against it.
45. Encouraging entrepreneurship among youth.
46. Setting up more educational institutes for agricultural and related studies.
47. Reverse brain drain.
48. Implementation of Uniform Civil code.
49. Balanced urban and rural development.
50. 100% literacy rate across India, not just Kerala.
51. Respect for all cultures, religions and genders.
52. No communal disputes or riots.
53. More fast-track courts to resolve legal matters quickly and efficiently.
54. Putting a stop to unnecessary expenditure on election campaigns.
55. Complete abolition of child labour. More awareness on 'Child abuse'.
56. Indian politicians need to refrain from being offensive and abusive, be it in speeches or on social media.
57. India must change its attitude towards debate and give up the policy of disruption.
58. Active participation in politics from the educated class and the youth. We need the educated to run the country, not the uninformed and hypocrites.
59. Society must learn to accept sexually abused victims.
60. More Wi-Fi enabled zones across the nation.
61. Well-organised emergency services at accident sites. Strict laws on drinking and driving should be passed.
62. Removal of unnecessary taxes. Thanks to the GST, we are in a better place now.

63. Cutting down the extravagant benefits given to the politicians or the people in power.
64. Improving the condition of slums.
65. Shelters for stray animals.
66. Affordable home facilities for the underprivileged.
67. Cleaning of all rivers in India.
68. Doing away with the "Chalta Hai" attitude.
69. Promotion of Indian culture in the real sense.

Don't listen to retarded politicians, and you're good to go. Remember - The most hateful, violent, ignorant, misogynistic, racist and unscientific sh*t has always been said in front of a flag that people love and on a stage that was built by taking money from the very people the stage is going to oppress. Mic drop.

CHAPTER EIGHT

HOW TO PENCIL OUT THE PERFECT WAY FOR EXISTENCE?

"Jo duniya ko namumkin lage,
  wahi mauka hai,
  Kartab dikhane ka."

This chapter is going to be in the form of a short story. It can be enjoyed to the fullest if all the five sections are thoroughly read one after the other. Enough of the introduction, here it goes-

When the pencil was made for the first time, the pencil maker gave the pencil some very crucial, pertinent and important instructions, which can actually give us very inspiring lessons to be applied in our own lives. The first instruction that the pencil maker gave the pencil was, "What's truly significant actually lies within you".

The pencil has two aspects to it: the outside, which is its beautiful, colourful, wooden casing and the inside, which is the lead, its very substance, it's very purpose. Similarly, in our lives as well, we have the outside. The outside is about our personality, our looks, our presence. I firmly believe that no one looks as good as their Instagram pictures, and no one looks as ugly as their Aadhaar Card picture. The inside is about being a genuine, sincere person. The outside is about charisma, our style, our presentation, how we speak, our confidence, our mannerisms. The inside is about our character, our morals, our integrity, the principles that we hold sacred in our lives. The outside is about valuables. In the world today, we are accepted more for what we have than who we are. We are accepted for what we wear rather than for who we are. We are accepted more for what we drive than who we are. Not only that, but we are accepted more today for where we live than who we are.

Valuables seem to be so crucial and overly emphasised in modern society. The outside is about valuables. The inside is about our values. Friends, while we focus on the outside, we shouldn't forget the inside. There's a great need to find that right balance. We live in the real world, so the outside is important. But our focus on the outside should never be at the cost of our inner world. Material education teaches us how to develop our outside, our externals, all our skills, our talent, which can buy us all the valuables to live in the real world. Spiritual education teaches us how to focus on the inside world. And therefore, there is such a great need to find that fine balance between our personality and being a genuine person, between our charisma and our character, between our valuables and our values.

Yes, the first instruction that the pencil maker gave the pencil was, "What's of true importance lies within you". And yes, what's of true importance lies within us. Our being a person, our character, our values, our very essence and the wonderful qualities of our soul.

The second amazing thing that the pencil maker told the pencil was, "Unless what is within you (the lead) comes out, you cannot make an impact". It's only when the lead comes out of the casing can the pencil actually make an impact on the paper by writing something.

Similarly, in our lives as well, unless what is within us comes out, we will not be able to make an impact, either on our own lives or on those of others. Thus, the Latin word *educare* from which the English word 'education' is derived means "to bring out", to bring out the virtues, the qualities of our soul. Yes, our personality can impress, but being a true person can inspire. Yes, our charisma can impress, but our character can inspire others. Yes, the valuables we possess can truly impress the world, but the values that we hold and live by can inspire the lives of others. In order to make an impact, we need to live by those sacred values, principles and ethics which are the very essentials of our core, our souls.

Each of us certainly remembers that one person, either our teacher, our friend or someone in the world who by being such an amazing person has made that impact on our lives. And we could be that incredible person to make an impact on someone's life by our inspiring example.

Yes, the second instruction that the pencil maker gave the pencil was, "When what is inside comes out, it can truly make an impact".

The fourth thing that the pencil maker told the pencil was, "When you write, you will most certainly end up making mistakes, what's truly great is that right behind you is attached an eraser, and you can actually correct that mistake at once and write the right thing". Even in our lives we make so many mistakes and what's amazing is that God has given us the opportunity, the chance to erase them, to correct them, and to rewrite our stories. We all make mistakes. Yes, we do. We should learn from them, erase and correct them, but never repeat them. And this is the fourth thing that the pencil maker told the pencil.

The fifth instruction that the pencil maker gave to the pencil was this; "You can truly serve your purpose when you are in the hands of an expert". In the hand of an expert artist, a beautiful sketch is made. In the hand of an expert architect, the pencil can make a construction plan. In the hands of an expert poet, writer, the pencil can write a poem or a story. When we act as instruments in the hands of God, our teachers, our mentors, our experienced trustworthy guides, we will be able to make an incredible impact on the world regardless of who we are and what colour we are. Some of us may be Americans, Indians or Russians. We may have different nationalities, different genders, different orientations, but in all probabilities, we can end up being of great value to humanity if we chose to be so. The externals truly do not matter. Our insides should be developed and act as instruments of grace. An equipoised, spiritually elevated soul will see, regardless of any externals, the true joy of life if he or she decides to do so.

CHAPTER NINE

LIFE AND THE ISSUES SURROUNDING IT

"Babumoshai zindagi badi honi chahiye, lambi nahi."

Before starting this chapter, I would like to add a section on the '**HUSTLE CULTURE**' that has engulfed all of us in the recent years-

Hustle means to do something in terms of working and grinding to achieve something insurmountable. It has become popular slang by these really famous motivation gurus on YouTube who sell you personality development courses for twenty-five grand or some absurd amount like that. Everyone talks about the fact that one must hustle 24*7 to achieve success.

Mark Manson with his book "The Subtle Art of Not Giving A F*ck" single-handedly converted the entire millennial generation into hustlers. Hustling seems more like a cult than a lifestyle. The peer pressure of being a hustler and getting work done faster is being prioritised more than just doing good work and enjoying the process. The concept of hustling has made the journey of hard work monotonous and the aim more important. However, I have contrary views on this topic. The journey has to be as exciting as the aim in mind, otherwise the aim just becomes mundane, and the eventual results don't fulfil one's heart.

When you are hustling, you are essentially saying that I want this so badly that I am willing to sacrifice everything for it. That tells you that there is a void that you are trying to fill by getting this. I generally think that there is no point to life anyway. So you create games, and you play the game extremely well. So if your game is to succeed, then just play the game. Your life's meaning is whatever you want it to be.

The point of life is to create goals, and you should only create goals which help you to attain flow. Let me explain the concept of flow in case one doesn't know what it is. 'Flow' is when the challenge that you pose to yourself and the skills that you have are matched. If the challenge is too difficult and that doesn't match your skill set, you become anxious. However, if your challenge is too easy and your skills overpower that, it'll be too easy, and you'll be stuck in boredom. 'Flow' is when there are good challenges and skills need to be exact to match it. And if your goals have flow, then you're likely to continue succeeding. And every time you achieve one goal, you have to find the next goal and be like: How can I find my flow in it.

One of the things that I've learnt over the last many years is that people in our country have a very zero-sum mentality. We believe that one person's success means that you're taking success from other people. People don't realise that everyone can be successful and everyone can make money. You just need to put your skill in the game and help yourself, and eventually everyone can succeed.

"Hustle Culture" is often defined as "No Sleep, All Work". The truth is- It's just about making sure that your actions match your ambitions. Easy.

Do I believe that work ethic is a foundational piece of success? Yes, I do.

Do I want anybody ever to work so much that they get burned out? Of Course Not.

Done with this section now. This was my take on hustle and productivity. I'm working on myself, and I still haven't figured all of it out. Hence, the length of this section is on the shorter side.

Life is a complex time when we grow up in the presence of our parents, get educated, find love (if luck does its work), get married, face the world, get objectified, get judged each day, have children, make money, have children, grow old, shift to Second Innings House (Lage Raho Munnabhai reference) and eventually perish in the very mud we were created from. How your life often goes also depends on the family you were born into. If you're born to the Ambanis and the Mittals, you grow up seeing your family run the country. On the other hand, if you are born to a farmer, you see the hardships and difficulties one faces day-to-day in order to survive. That's the beauty of our country, I think. No matter how well off you think you are, someone got it better than you. And no matter how miserable you think your life is, someone got it much worse. This realisation is the best thing that can happen to an individual in my opinion. And if it happens to you early on in your life, it would be even great.

The more life happens to you, the more naturally cynical you become because you realise that the world is a gloomy place. The only thing that helps you out in a bad situation is being positive. I used to think that this is all just 'gyaan' that people impart. I mean seriously I'm here failing my semester exams and all you can advise is "Ayan beta, be positive, everything happens for a reason". But slowly and steadily I have come to the realisation that over analysing the issues and getting sad by it takes you nowhere and makes you fall into depression. The ray of positivity, however small it may be, eventually is the only thing that helps you out in some form or manner.

We often measure wisdom as the number of years of experience, however, wisdom is the number of experiences in a year. Patience and the realisation that life is long, and you don't have to be in a hurry is important. Just keep working with sincerity and things will work out. They always do. For some people in the early part of their careers and for some a little later. But they do.

Be Patient and Be Positive. Greater things are on the way.

The other day I wrote this poem. I think that this can perfectly sum up life, at least that's what I think:

Life is so strange
Nothing stays the same
Everything change
But who to blame
Life is like a game
Where you have to lose
Before you can gain
To win, you have to face the fearful rain
In life... They always say
Don't use your heart

Only use your brain
In life, there is love
But the more is hate
No one decide
They all hesitate
And who knows the fate
The closest people you need go away
When you need them the most
You find them lost
Day after day
Days go by
People are born...and other die
Year after year
No one understands
Nothing is clear
Nothing in our hearts except fear
Today you walk and talk
Tomorrow you lay in your grave
And nothing it gave
The money that you save
And no use of your gold
When it won't be sold
You have to be strong
Stop doing the wrong
And never lie
Be ready for your last goodbye

We often look at **arrogance** as a bad thing. If someone takes too much pride in what they are great at, people assume that the person is arrogant. The second you start looking at arrogance as a bad thing, what's actually happening is that you are being envious of someone and judging them, and that's not necessarily good. If you think of someone as arrogant, you are being judgemental. Secondly, most arrogance is largely a manifestation of its projection. No one means to be arrogant. It's just that they are inherently insecure that they just double down their qualities. I think people don't realise their flaws and everyone feels that he or she is an idiot, and you do anything to reflect the opposite, and that just ends up being the arrogance that people witness. People are not arrogant because they want others to feel good. People are arrogant because they want to protect their own self-esteem.

So am I saying arrogance is good? Absolutely not. It's the worst. But we should change our definitions of arrogance as we go about in our lives.

Confidence is one of the best traits one can have, arrogance is one of the worst. And the line between the two can be blurry. Some people are worried that if they become confident, they'll cross the line into arrogance or even if they don't, other people will perceive their newly found confidence as arrogance.

Being too arrogant can be an obstacle to our well-being and our interpersonal relationships because not being able to dominate pride can become a problem for natural communication and the expression of our feelings. Also, being very proud does not allow us to recognize our mistakes and makes us blame others for our own failures. I can think of five solutions to this 'Arrogance Problem'. Here it goes-

1. <u>Do not get offended so easily</u> - If you are looking for reasons to feel offended, you'll find the ones you want. This way of thinking makes you weaker, as it causes you to be continually defensive and wasting your mental

energy with unnecessary confrontations. Instead, adopt another way of thinking and accept both others and yourself, because feeling offended by everything that happens around you will only make it difficult to coexist with the others. Ne humble, be compassionate and move on with life.

2. <u>Identify, acknowledge and stop thinking about what they think of you</u> - Being too prideful can be difficult to detect many times because it is not easy to reflect on what we do not do well. Insecurity, fear of failure or fear of being judged are often behind this behaviour. The first step is to identify that we are very prideful, and recognize that there are situations in which that can play against us. Only in this way can we behave differently. Achieving inner peace and not letting yourself be affected by what others think of you can help you be more humble and improve your relationships with people around you.

3. <u>Get rid of the need to always be right</u> - The constant need to always want to be right can cause you to stop being objective. On many occasions, we want to defend our point of view without reflecting on the point of view of others. Remember that not everyone thinks the same way you do, and that different truths can exist depending on the point of view from which you look. Also, even if you do not share the thoughts of another person, you can accept it equally because people also have the right to make mistakes. Living in a state of constant competition against others can be very exhausting and very harmful for you. Showing yourself open to the opinion of others and listening to them will greatly benefit you.

4. <u>Overcome the need to feel superior to others</u> - Constantly improving has nothing to do with wanting to be superior to others. Personal development is born from the desires and the internal tastes of each one, not from the approval of others. Wanting to judge everyone because of their appearance, their possessions or their achievements makes a lot of sense to feed the ego, but it is detrimental from the point of view of mental well-being. Dividing people between winners and losers, honestly, is pretty sad. This way of thinking leads to hostility, resentment, and confrontation, and in the long term, this mentality will distance you from other subjects instead of approaching them, because you will always see them as your rivals. This need to feel superior to others will cause you to be inflexible, so you can start by being humble and stop wanting to feel superior to the rest. Accept yourself as you are: with your virtues and your faults.

5. <u>Give a touch of humour to life</u> - Putting a sense of humour in conflicts will improve your relationships with people around you. Try to be compassionate to others and laugh at the problems. There is nothing better than talking about things with humour to de-stress and look at life with less anguish.

Overthinking is simply the act of "thinking about something too much or for too long". It is energy draining, it elevates our stress level, reduces our creativity, clouds our judgement and strips us of our power to make decisions.

Overthinking is a real thing. We all tend to overthink. And strangely, it's almost always about the things that will go bad. I don't think that anyone in history was overthinking about the good that can happen. It's always those depressing thoughts that capture our brains.

Like, imagine your friend calling you at midnight right before an interview the next day and going like, "Oh My God Dude, I can't stop overthinking. Are they gonna love me, are they gonna fall for my credentials and my degree? Surely I will get the job and earn a lot". This stuff never happens. What actually happens is: "Oh My God, Dude, I can't stop overthinking. They're gonna reject me. I only have this interview lined up. I have already quit my previous job. And if I don't get this one, I don't know what I'm going to do. I will go broke, and my girlfriend will leave me. My mother is going to get me fixed for an arranged marriage. Sh*t". We're hardwired to think about the bad more than the good. That's what it is.

If you are always thinking about how beautiful and amazing the world is, how grateful you are and how much love there is around you, would you ever want to stop thinking about that? No, of course not. You're never overthinking the positive because if you did then you would never stop doing that. You are always thinking about the negatives, which means that you are focusing on the wrong things. Too many problems and too many situations led us to this point. So, how to frame the issues in such a narrow way that we get the answer? That's the question which needs to be answered.

Remember that day when you didn't have a single thought?

Yeah. Neither does anyone else.

We are perpetual thinkers. It's a non-stop habit. You generate about seventy thousand thoughts per day. What are these thoughts about? Are they helping you live the life that you want to live? Or are they making you feel less about yourself and others?

The solution is: You must actually become aware of what is going on inside your head. And that sounds simple enough. But many of us never realise that there's some negative stuff happening out there. And instead we choose to act like everything is okay. Are you overthinking? Are you thinking negatively? Well, admit it because otherwise you won't be able to change a thing. Self-improvement begins with self acceptance. When you actually make it clear to yourself that you don't like what's going on, and you begin to get aware of it, you can start to make a real change. You can keep a thought journal, writing down your thoughts as they come up. At least the more noticeable ones. Even if they're negative, it'll help you to start to get an overview of what's cooking up in your mind. And after this, it'll be much easier to make the changes you want to make because you'll know what's actually going on.

Another solution: Use Meditation. Yeah, use it. When you train your mind with a simple technique like focusing on your breathing for ten minutes per day and repeating it every time you get distracted, you start to get power over your mind. Understand also that if you do not train your mind, it is guaranteed to run wild on you. Like a crazy chimp, it'll mess up your state of mind and in the end it'll mess up your life. So control it. Use meditation because it works, and don't be discouraged if you can't seem to stay focused in the beginning. Simply stay disciplined and continue to practise. This is one of the very best and most effective ways to beat overthinking, and it will absolutely work for you as long as you stay with it.

Now that I've started sounding like those YouTube motivation gurus, which I despise, I should pull up an interesting story to make this conversation a bit more fun and relaxed.

<u>Here goes the story</u>:

An artist once came to a King who was a great admirer of art and said, "Oh, King! If you give me a blank wall in your palace, I can create a spectacular painting on it".

Just then, another young man, who was present there, said to the King, "Your Majesty! Please allow me to work on the opposite wall. I am an artist too".

The King asked the young man, "And what would you like to make?".

The man said, "I shall make an exact replica of the painting that the other artist makes on the wall opposite to mine. And I shall do so without even looking at his work. I would request you to place a thick curtain between the two walls so that neither of us can see the other's work, and also have guards to make sure that there is no foul play".

Everyone in the court, including the King, was intrigued, and the King decided to give both artists the opportunity to show their talent.

The following day, a thick curtain was put in the palace and both the artists started their work.

The first artist brought paints and oils and brushes that he worked with. The second one worked simply with a cloth and a bucket of water.

After a month, the first artist told the King that his work was complete and when the King asked the second artist about his status, the young man replied that he was done too.

The King came to the palace and went on to see the first artist's wall. He was stunned by the spectacular painting and gave the artist a hefty sum as a reward.

He then asked for the curtain to be opened up to see if the second artist had met up with the challenge of creating the exact same painting without seeing it.

The curtain opened and lo and behold! On the opposite wall was an exact replica of the painting.

Every single line, every single colour, every minor detail was exactly as it was on the first wall.

The King rewarded the man with double the amount of money, but being amused and wanted to know his secret.

The young artist replied, "It was very simple, Your Majesty!, I just polished the marble wall every day, until it shone like a mirror to reflect the painting on the opposite wall".

Story commences.

All of these are a part of you. The hard work is cleaning the wall of your mind in a way that what's hidden deep within you, your talent, your positivity, your confidence, your goodness is reflected in your mind and thus in your actions, and then you can indeed achieve something spectacular.

Don't they say that the soul knows how to heal itself?

The challenge is to silence the mind. And one of the ways to silence the mind's negative chatter is to neglect it.

And how does one ignore the chatter?

By absorbing the mind in positive energy. Reading, hearing, listening or watching positive stuff. Hanging out with positive people. And then as the mind becomes slowly cleansed, the beautiful painting within you will be reflected on it.

That's all.

Ending the chapter on a Sadhguru quote: "Happiness is not about getting what you like. Happiness has a lot to do with liking what you get".

Finishing The Book

I started writing this book back in 2019. Due to some reasons, I scrapped the idea of continuing it after a week.

2020 came and then we all knew what happened. COVID happened.

Our Prime Minster came on our television screens once again and announced a twenty-one-day lockdown, which eventually dragged throughout the year. The initial months, particularly, were quite depressing. Productivity dropped to zero, and binge-watching became a thing. I remember that I used to sleep whenever I wanted, waking up at odd hours became the new normal. Streaming an entire web show through the day was not a big thing any more.

But these things got really old really quickly. And one day I decided to continue writing. Initially, I planned to release this book in 2021. But by the end of 2020, I got really busy with my college examinations and other chores at hand. The book got pushed back again.

Eventually, in the last quarter of 2021, I decide to complete the book. As I went through some of the pages I had written in the last year, I realized that it would qualify more like a rant rather than a book. I restarted writing all over again in September 2021 and completed the final draft at the end of December.

I'm happy to see that the book is finally published.

This is the paperback version of the book. Hopefully the Kindle edition will be available fairly soon.

I'm also planning to upload an audiobook version of the same on Audible. Stay tuned for lots more.

For any queries, mail me - hasanayan263@gmail.com

With Love

Somewhere between neurons and narratives,
    I was born,
    lived (dreamt)
    &
    died.

          -Sushant Singh Rajput (1986 - 2020)

www.ingramcontent.com/pod-product-compliance
Lightning Source LLC
Chambersburg PA
CBHW020724160726
47993CB00006B/2337